THE *CONFESSION* OF
MIKHAIL BAKUNIN

Mikhail Aleksandrovich Bakunin in the 1860s

THE *CONFESSION* OF MIKHAIL BAKUNIN

with the marginal comments of Tsar Nicholas I

translated by

ROBERT C. HOWES

introduction and notes by

LAWRENCE D. ORTON

Cornell University Press ITHACA AND LONDON

First published 1977 by Cornell University Press.
Published in the United Kingdom by Cornell University Press Ltd.,
2-4 Brook Street, London W1Y 1AA.

International Standard Book Number 0-8014-1073-8
Library of Congress Catalog Card Number 76-25646
Printed in the United States of America by Vail-Ballou Press, Inc.
Librarians: Library of Congress cataloging information appears on the last page of the book.

CONTENTS

ACKNOWLEDGMENTS

We wish to express our appreciation to Arthur Lehning of the Internationaal Instituut voor Sociale Geschiedenis (Amsterdam) and Melvin Cherno of Oakland University for their helpful advice and encouragement. We are also indebted to Marian Wilson for her expert editorial assistance and invaluable counsel.

R. C. H.
L. D. O.

Rochester, Michigan

TRANSLATOR'S NOTE

This translation of Bakunin's *Confession* is based upon the text of the document as it appears in *M. Λ. Bakunin: Sobranie sochinenii i pisem, 1828–1876*, edited by Iu. M. Steklov, 4 vols., vol. IV: *V tiur'makh i ssylke, 1848–1861* (1935; reprint Düsseldorf and Vaduz, 1970).

I have also compared the Steklov version with the text of the *Confession* in *Materialy dlia biografii M. Bakunina*, edited by Viacheslav Polonskii, 3 vols. (Moscow and Petrograd/ Leningrad, 1923–1933).

Discrepancies between the two texts have been noted, but I have chosen to rely on Steklov's editing as definitive.

R. C. H.

INTRODUCTION

Your former acquaintance, D'iakova's brother, is living here on the very bank of the Neva and is now writing his memoirs, not of course for publication, but for the sovereign. He is setting matters straight in a most intelligent manner, wily as a serpent; he is extricating himself from the most difficult circumstances—now by gibes at the Germans, now by openhearted repentance, and now by rapturous praise. Indeed, he is clever.

[A lady of the court to her cousin Katerina Ivanovna, 1851]

And now I turn again to my Sovereign, and, falling at the feet of Your Imperial Majesty, I implore you: Sire! I am a great criminal and do not deserve forgiveness!

[Mikhail Bakunin, *Confession*]

I am alive, I am well, I am strong, I am getting married, I am happy, I love and remember you, and, to you as well as to myself, I remain unalterably true.

[Mikhail Bakunin to A. I. Herzen, Tomsk, summer 1858] [1]

What prompted Mikhail Aleksandrovich Bakunin, the most celebrated of Russia's nineteenth-century revolutionaries, to "confess" to Tsar Nicholas I, the "gendarme of Europe"? This question has puzzled generations of admirers and detractors, biographers and historians, and even now, a century after Bakunin's death, a conclusive answer still eludes us.

Born in 1814—the very year that Russian armies triumphantly entered Paris to depose Napoleon—Mikhail, a child of Russia's privileged nobility and the eldest son among ten children, grew up on the family estate of Priamukhino in the province of Tver, not far from Moscow. As a youth he was apparently quite happy until at the age of fourteen he was sent by his father (who, in the wake of the Decembrist revolt, had given up his liberal European views and become an ardent admirer of Nicholas I) to the Artillery Cadet School in St. Petersburg. Having grown up in the company of his adoring sisters, Bakunin never adjusted to the austere, regimented atmosphere of the military school. He was commissioned an ensign in 1833, and after his dismissal from the academy about a year later there came a brief and equally unhappy assignment to an artillery brigade in the Lithuanian borderlands of the empire. Then, in 1835, he quit the army and returned to Priamukhino, leaving to his father the chore of averting a public scandal over this apparent desertion.

Between 1835 and his departure for Berlin at the age of twenty-six, two passions infused Bakunin's life: an infatuation with German metaphysics and the platonic, possessive love he shared with his sisters. The young Mikhail exuded a magnetic attraction that he used to dominate his sisters' lives. To his father's mounting annoyance, Mikhail refused to accept a post in the civil service, preferring to shuttle between Priamukhino and Moscow, where the latest works of the German philosophers were devoured by small circles of passionately romantic devotees. In these circles the personal magnetism and will to dominate that Bakunin had displayed in Priamukhino gained sway over two young intellectuals in particular, Nikolai Stankevich and Vissarion Belinsky.

Bakunin and his friends took little interest in political matters, so consumed were they in discovering the higher purposes and meaning of life. Even friendship with Alexander Herzen, who had been arrested and briefly banished from Moscow for his political radicalism, failed to awaken in Bakunin any outrage over Russia's social conditions. As he himself expressed it in 1838 in his introduction to a collection of Hegel's lectures: "To revolt against reality means to kill in oneself the living source of life. . . . Let us hope that the new generation will reconcile itself with our beautiful Russian reality." [2]

But soon his quarrels with Belinsky, the illness of Stankevich, and the death of his sister Liubov turned an increasingly lonely Bakunin inward. He closeted himself at Priamukhino, seldom visited Moscow, and read voraciously. His urge to dominate was temporarily submerged in a thirst for knowledge. His overriding goal was to study in Berlin, at the fountainhead of Hegelian thought. In 1840 he composed a lengthy apology to his father, in which he begged forgiveness for the many upsets he had caused the family and pleaded for funds to permit him to study abroad. Aleksandr Bakunin, now in failing health, finally agreed to provide his eldest son with the means to live abroad. In June 1840 Mikhail sailed from St. Petersburg.

The *Confession* covers Bakunin's life from his arrival in Berlin to his arrest in 1849. He describes his disillusionment with German idealist philosophy and his gradual conversion into an "absolute democrat." In his journey across Western Europe after leaving Berlin in 1842—first to Dresden, then to Zurich, Brussels, and Paris—Bakunin became acquainted with German political exiles (including Marx, whom he disliked), Poles who had emigrated after the abortive 1830–1831 insurrection against tsarist domination, a handful of Russians, and French opponents of the July Monarchy. Bakunin was introduced to the budding strains of European socialism and communism but did not ally himself with any particular movement. Not until 1847 did the fervor of revolutionary mission grip him. He first placed his hopes on the Polish revolutionaries, whose struggle, he proclaimed, must be joined to the liberation of Russia from tsarist tyranny. But his collaboration with the Poles was hampered by persistent but unfounded rumors that this itinerant Russian revolutionary, who lived without visible means of support, was in fact a tsarist agent—a suspicion fostered by the Russian authorities.

The February Revolution of 1848 found Bakunin in Brussels. He hastened to Paris to share in the euphoric first days of the newly proclaimed French Republic. The tide of revolution across Europe in the spring of 1848 rekindled Bakunin's hopes for revolution in his homeland. His goal was the Duchy of Poznań, from which he hoped to carry the banner of revolt to Russian Poland. The Prussian authorities, however, permitted him to travel only as far as Breslau, where he learned of the Slav Congress in Prague. Momentarily disillusioned with the course of the revolution in German Central Europe, Bakunin was aroused by a vision of Slav unity. He hurried to Prague to expound his program for Slav federation and to share the Slavs' growing distrust of German expansionism. When the congress was disrupted by the ill-fated popular revolt against the authoritarian Austrian military commander Prince Alfred zu Windischgrätz, Bakunin briefly joined the fighting on the barricades before making good his escape. Returning to Germany, he was hounded by the Prussian and Saxon authorities, but soon found a haven in the constitutionally liberal enclave of Anhalt-Köthen. At the close of 1848 he wrote an inflammatory *Appeal to the Slavs,* in which he urged Austria's Slavs to set aside national passions and unite with the German and Magyar democrats to block the rising tide of counterrevolution.

In 1849 Bakunin conspired with a handful of German and Czech radicals, but their plots miscarried and in May he was captured by the Saxon police, tried, and sentenced to death. Later the sentence was commuted to life imprisonment, and he was handed over to the Austrians, who had been seeking him for his part in the unsuccessful insurrection in Prague. In Habsburg hands Bakunin endured a similar ordeal: interrogation and trial, ending with a death sentence, followed by commutation of sentence. This time, at the request of Tsar Nicholas, Bakunin was delivered to Russian officials, who in 1844 had sentenced him *in absentia* to loss of his gentry status and privileges and to penal servitude in Siberia for refusing to obey the summons to return to Russia.

Back in Russia, Bakunin was neither tried nor sent to Siberia but placed in solitary confinement in the Peter and Paul Fortress in St. Petersburg while the tsar pondered his fate. For two months nothing happened; then Bakunin was visited by Count Aleksei Fedorovich Orlov, head of the political police, who suggested that he write an account of his transgressions for the tsar. "Tell him that he should write to me as a spiritual son writes to his spiritual father," Nicholas had instructed Orlov.[3]

Bakunin's motives in complying with this invitation are still disputed. In his only written reference to the Confession, Bakunin explained his reaction to Herzen:

I thought a little and reflected that before a jury in an open trial I would have to play out my role to the end, but that, within four walls in the power of the bear, I could without shame soften my stance, and therefore I demanded a month's time, agreed, and actually wrote a sort of confession, something in the nature of a Dichtung und Wahrheit.* My activities had in any case been so open that there was nothing for me to hide. . . . After this, à quelques exceptions près,† I recounted to Nicholas my entire life abroad with all my plans, impressions, and feelings, and was unable to resist offering many instructive remarks concerning his internal and foreign policies. My letter—taking into account, first, the clarity of my obviously hopeless situation and, second, the strong personality of Nicholas—was written very firmly and boldly, and precisely for this reason greatly pleased him.[4]

One searches in vain through Bakunin's correspondence and writings for further mention of his reasons and intentions in addressing himself to Nicholas.

After accepting the tsar's invitation, Bakunin was provided with pen and paper. It is likely that he wrote in the same manner in which he had pursued the elusive banner of revolution across Europe—in a flurry of frantic activity, punctuated with periods of despondency and lethargy. Working from memory, without notes, he filled ninety-six pages and, to judge from the original, made remarkably few corrections. How long did Bakunin take to complete his letter to the tsar? If we accept his statement that Orlov first entered his cell two months after his incarceration (11/23 May 1851) and that, according to Count

* Poetry and Truth (the title of Goethe's autobiography).
† With a few exceptions.

Dubel't, the deputy head of the Third Section, the *Confession*
was delivered to Nicholas on 13 August (old style), then he
probably worked for about the one month he had requested of
Orlov. Nicholas did not read Bakunin's original manuscript; a
second copy was specially prepared by a Third Section calli-
grapher to spare the tsar the effort of deciphering Bakunin's
tiny, irregular handwriting. That Nicholas read the document
carefully is evidenced not only by his numerous marginal
comments, but by the notation he made at the head of the first
page for his son, the future Alexander II: "You should read
this through, it's very interesting and instructive." Who else
read the *Confession?* Certainly only those persons Nicholas believed the most trustworthy: Orlov, Dubel't, and Prince Aleksandr Ivanovich Chernyshev, who headed the State Council. It
was also sent to General Ivan Fedorovich Paskevich, the Russian governor of Poland, to determine whether Bakunin had
provided any information that might be useful in keeping
watch on the troublesome Poles.[5]

The *Confession* was not immediately consigned to the re-
cesses of the Third Section archives. In 1857, when Bakunin's
family was imploring the tsar to moderate Mikhail's sentence,
Alexander II purportedly confronted his foreign minister,
Prince Aleksandr Mikhailovich Gorchakov, with the *Confession,* remarking, "Mais je ne vois pas le moindre repentir dans
cette lettre" ("But I do not see the slightest repentance in this
letter"). In a letter to Herzen, Bakunin wrote, "The fool
wanted *repentir!*" [6]

There is also strong evidence that on at least one occasion
the Russian authorities were prepared to use the *Confession* to
compromise Bakunin's standing in revolutionary circles after
his subsequent escape from Siberia. At the time of the 1863
Polish insurrection, Bakunin traveled to Sweden to join a Polish émigré project for a seaborne assault on Russia's Baltic
possessions (the stillborn Ward Jackson affair). The idea of ex-
posing Bakunin probably stemmed from the public attack on
him by the Swedish foreign minister, Count Manderstrøm, to
which Bakunin had brashly replied in a Swedish newspaper
that "there was not a single fact in my past life for which I

need blush." [7] The Third Section thereupon concocted a brochure, "Mikhail Bakunin, Depicted by Himself," which contained "incriminating" passages from the *Confession*. To add credibility, authorship was attributed to an anonymous Swede who, while working in the Russian archives on Russo-Swedish relations, had unearthed these remarkable papers by Bakunin. The aim of the tsarist authorities was the same as it had been in 1847 and 1848, when they fabricated rumors that Bakunin was a tsarist agent in order to discredit him in the eyes of his fellow revolutionaries. The Swedish government cooperated with the Russian authorities to neutralize an embarrassing agitator in their country who might upset Sweden's cherished neutrality. The manuscript for the brochure was submitted to Alexander II on 12 June 1863 for his approval, but, inexplicably, the project was shelved.[8] Perhaps the tsar now felt that the attendant publicity would attract attention to the Russians' failure to keep this dangerous revolutionary in custody. It is not known whether Bakunin was personally threatened with disclosure of the *Confession* by either Manderstrøm or the Russian minister in Stockholm, Count Dashkov. In any case, he did leave Sweden precipitously and subsequently broke off contact with the Poles, a circumstance that has led a few writers to speculate that he was coerced into abandoning his revolutionary schemes.[9] Most authors agree, however, that Bakunin's plans for collaboration with the Poles had already gone awry and that he left Sweden of his own volition.[10]

Did the Russian authorities ever use "Mikhail Bakunin, Depicted by Himself" to threaten their celebrated opponent at a later date? There is no conclusive evidence that they did, but it is difficult to believe that they would forgo such a weapon, especially since the passage of time would have made Bakunin's action of 1851 all the more difficult to justify to the new revolutionary generation of the sixties and seventies.[11]

Although the *Confession* was not made public during Bakunin's lifetime, there is little doubt that its existence haunted him. Apparently he was often questioned about it in later years. That he regretted writing the document is strongly indicated by his remarks to Zamfir Ralli, his anarchist companion of later years:

It was a great mistake on my part; in my letter I expressed much truth to Nicholas, but all the while I related to him as to a man who loves Russia, and this I should not have done because Nicholas was a f[ool] * and he could not understand me. I would give much if this letter did not exist. . . . It was Slavophile; at that time I assigned too much significance to Russia in the matter of liberating the Slavs from the German yoke. It was written under the influence of the outrages I had endured in Austrian prisons. [12]

Ralli's recollections of Bakunin's remarks deserve particular attention, since they were recorded before the contents of the *Confession* became known. Less credible are the contentions of several anarchists made after the publication of the *Confession*. For instance, in an anarchist tribute to Bakunin published in Berlin in 1926, Mikhail P. Sazhin (Arman Ross) asserted that Bakunin had nothing to hide and had freely divulged to him the real nature of the *Confession*. [13] It was also alleged that Petr Kropotkin had been shown the document and had found nothing remarkable about it. [14]

To be sure, before the 1917 revolutions in Russia, the existence of the *Confession* was widely known, although not by that name. As early as 1895, in the introduction to Bakunin's published correspondence, the Ukrainian writer Myhailo Drahomaniv had speculated that Bakunin's "report" to Nicholas might be found "in the now seemingly accessible archives of the Third Section." [15] The particular section where the *Confession* was kept, however, was hardly accessible. The first scholar known to have had a glimpse of the *Confession* was the distinguished German Russianist Theodor Schiemann, on the eve of World War I. Though he was not permitted to examine the document itself, he was shown Orlov's correspondence of July and August 1851 with the tsar, which shed important light on Nicholas' purpose in having Bakunin write the *Confession*. After relaying the tsar's invitation to Bakunin, Orlov

* In the Russian original, published in 1908, Ralli wrote "d . . .","" which from the spacing and context presumably stands for *durak*", fool.

reported to his master: "I spoke at some length . . . with Bakunin and related to him precisely what you were pleased to command me. I found him well composed. It seems that he is nearly ready to repent, and he has begun today to write down his experiences and has promised to hold back nothing. But he did request that he be allowed time to explain everything thoroughly." A month later, when Orlov delivered the completed confession to Nicholas, he added his own note:

I am sending Bakunin's written statement, which I read with great attention. . . . He reports in detail and candidly on all events and on his relations with the republican leaders. Fortunately, he had no contacts in Russia. As to his wish to be assigned to forced labor instead of remaining in the fortress, Bakunin is a highly dangerous person and, I believe, not fully cured of his wrongheaded opinions. It seems to me, therefore, that Your Majesty ought not ultimately to determine his fate by your good heart. But I consider it possible in time to accord him, in mercy, a better arrangement within the fortress and to give him the possibility of breathing fresh air and later of seeing his relatives. But in no way should he be consigned to hard labor, where, because of his fiery and determined spirit, he would be dangerous and disruptive. Excuse my plain speaking, Your Majesty; it is my duty.

After reading the confession, Nicholas informed Orlov: "I entirely share your opinion. One cannot deal with him otherwise. He does not merit credence. I believe that for the time being he can continue to stay where he is." [16]

Orlov's messages to Nicholas suggest that Bakunin may not have composed his statement freely, but may in fact have been given specific questions, verbally or possibly in writing, to which Nicholas expected full and honest replies. Also, several passages intimate that Bakunin was asked for detailed information on certain subjects; for example, he writes, "But first I must answer the question," and "I have told everything, Sire, and, no matter how hard I think, I cannot find a single circumstance of even slight importance that I have omitted here," and "I have tried to put down . . . all my sins and not forget anything essential." What did Nicholas hope to learn from his celebrated captive? Certainly the intentions of the Pan-Slav and German nationalist movements, whose aims could bear on Russia's foreign policy; and especially the plottings of the Polish émigrés, who were a continual annoyance to Nicholas' gendarmes. But the tsar was probably most interested in Bakunin's revolutionary aims for Russia and in his relations with Russian opposition groups at home and abroad.[17] Such a concern would help to explain Orlov's obvious relief that Bakunin had apparently lacked ties within Russia for his various schemes.

Even when the files of the Third Section became accessible, publication of the *Confession* was hampered by political intrigues. In 1917 Professor L. Il'inskii submitted the manuscript to the Kadet (Constitutional Democratic) journal *Golos minuvshego*, which turned it down. The moderate editors apparently deemed the *Confession* too damaging a weapon to place in the hands of the Marxist parties. How could the anarchists and Socialist Revolutionaries—Bakunin's spiritual heirs—justify his apparently lapsed revolutionary integrity? Not until 1919 did Il'inskii manage to publish selected excerpts in *Vestnik literatury*.[18] It was not until 1921, after the consolidation of Bolshevik power, that the full text was published.[19] Two years later, Viacheslav Polonskii, editor of the 1921 edition, reprinted the *Confession* in a more authoritative version in the first volume of his source collection, *Materials for a Biography of M. Bakunin*.[20] Although several translations soon appeared (German, 1926;[21] Czech, 1926;[22] and French, 1932[23]), this intriguing document was not fully rendered into English.[24] In 1936 the Russian text was reprinted in Volume IV of Iurii M. Steklov's exhaustive collection of Bakunin's correspondence and writings (to 1861), where a number of errors in Polonskii's editions were corrected.[25]

The publication in 1919 of excerpts from the *Confession* caused immediate reverberations. As Peter Scheibert notes, "The effect was enormous: the great martyr of the revolutionary struggle, the theoretician of anarchism, had bowed before the embodiment of tyranny."[26] A heated polemical exchange ensued, a combination of apology and accusation that attempted to explain Bakunin's motives. The greatest con-

sternation centered on the obsequious tone of Bakunin's pre-
sentation. His strident denunciation of Western Europe's
evolving democratic institutions, his contempt for all things
German—including most of the German revolutionaries—and
especially his intimation of a common bond between tsar and
revolutionary startled contemporary readers.

The attack on Bakunin was launched by the renegade Russian anarchist Victor Serge (Kibalchich), now a Bolshevik apol-
ogist. In an article published in French and German Marxist
journals, Serge maintained that the *Confession* showed Bakunin to be a beaten man who clearly took bitter pleasure in
abasing himself before the tsar.[27] Serge accepted at face value
Bakunin's profuse contrition, suggesting that his about-face
may have stemmed from deep disappointment over the failure
of his 1848–1849 revolutionary dreams. Serge seized on Bakunin's passage concerning the need for dictatorial rule in
Russia, suggesting that "already in 1848 Bakunin had presaged
Bolshevism." Like later critics, Serge pointed to those Russian
revolutionaries, such as Nikolai Chernyshevsky, who endured
decades of tsarist imprisonment but refused to divulge anything to their captors.

Serge's evaluation of the *Confession* infuriated Max Nettlau,
the historian of anarchism and a biographer of Bakunin.
Nettlau, who vehemently denounced Serge's campaign to defile Bakunin's memory,[28] believed that Bakunin's purpose was
to "deceive the tyrant who was the master of his destiny." He
argued that Bakunin relished the chance to retrace his revolutionary schemes for the tsar (while never compromising his as-
sociates); but "at intervals he remembers his present situation
and throws to the tsar a few sops on sinning, foolishness,
quixotism, and the like, which are mere byplay, to keep up
the fiction agreed upon of a 'confession.' " Nettlau dismisses
Bakunin's submissive tone, noting that "the tsar would not
look at a document where these forms were neglected." In a
subsequent article, Nettlau maintained that the only honest element in the *Confession*, but perhaps Bakunin's major short-
coming, was its excessive Slav nationalism.[29]

Within Soviet Russia, however, the initial tendency was to

accept Bakunin's *Confession* as sincere. In the introduction to the first complete Russian edition, Polonskii saw in the *Confession* a reversion to Bakunin's former Hegelian views of Russia's "reasonable" reality. Helpless and alone in prison, but back at last in his native Russia, he saw only folly in his opinions and actions while he had been abroad.[30] Vera Figner, a former terrorist and a veteran of tsarist jails, likewise discerned an atavistic strain running through the *Confession;* there could be no question of pretense in its pages. But tragically, in Figner's view, Bakunin debased not only his own past but the revolutionary generation of the 1840s as well.[31]

B. P. Koz'min, in reviewing the *Confession,* also agreed that Bakunin's contrition was unfeigned, though he attributed this posture not to any psychic reversion but to Bakunin's despondency over the failure of the 1848–1849 struggles. Bakunin's expressed wish in the *Confession* that Nicholas would don the mantle of "people's tsar" (*zemskii tsar'*) and head a revolutionary dictatorship of the Slavs was not surprising to Koz'min; its origin lay in Bakunin's deep disappointment with Western democracy.[32] To support his argument, Koz'min cited Bakunin's remarkable pamphlet *The People's Cause: Romanov, Pugachev, or Pestel,* written in 1862, in which he had put forth the view that the tsar, rather than a peasant firebrand (Pugachev) or a representative of the privileged intelligentsia (Pestel), could best lead the revolution.

We should most gladly of all follow Romanov, if Romanov could and would transform himself from a Petersburg Emperor into a National Tsar. We should gladly enroll under his standard because the Russian people still recognizes him and because his strength is concentrated, ready to act, and might become an irresistible strength if only he would give it a popular baptism. We would follow him because he *alone* could carry out and complete a great, peaceful revolution without shedding one drop of Russian or Slav blood.[33]

The strongest voice to argue against any sincerity in the *Confession* was, surprisingly, that of the Soviet Marxist scholar Iurii M. Steklov. In his opinion, Bakunin assumed the mask of deceit with the goal of reducing his sentence and eventually regaining his freedom to renew the revolutionary struggle.[34] On the whole, anarchist apologists for Bakunin shared Steklov's view that Bakunin's feigned remorse and subservience were simply necessary expedients to deceive the tsar. They also emphasized the fact that Bakunin never swerved from his pledge of silence concerning those comrades who were not already known to tsarist authorities.[35]

Most of the early commentators seemed to be searching for some clue to Bakunin's motives in agreeing to Nicholas' request. There was therefore a great stir occasioned by the discovery at Priamukhino of several letters that Bakunin had smuggled to his sister Tatiana during one of the rare visits of the family to the prison in 1854. When A. N. Kornilov published them in 1925, they provoked a startling change of opinion in a number of critics who had at first accepted Bakunin's sincerity.[36] What could Bakunin have written, three years *after* the *Confession*, to cause this remarkable about-face? Essentially, the letters depict an intensely suffering individual. Bakunin describes in detail his physical deterioration, the consequence of inactivity, foul air, and mental anguish. But he also attests to a burning desire to be "useful" once again, "to serve the sacred cause": "For me only one interest remains: a single object to which I cling, in which I believe . . . , and when I can no longer live for it, then I do not wish to live at all. . . . My moral state still holds well, and my head is clear in spite of the pain. My will—I hope that it never breaks. It seems that I never had so many thoughts, never felt such a fiery urge for movement and action. . . . All that remains for me in life is embodied in a single word: Freedom!"

Here, seemingly, lay the long-sought key. Bakunin's will had remained unbroken after all. But he could not stand a life devoid of hope and purpose, and so had employed the only available means—a ruse—to regain his liberty. So consumed had he been by this aim that he had paid no attention to the possible consequences of his act of "confession." From a position of total acceptance of Bakunin's candor a few years earlier, Polonskii now characterized the *Confession* as a "Machiavellian masterpiece." [37] Of course, for those who had doubted all along, the smuggled letters confirmed the belief that the revolutionary had simply feigned penitence.[38]

The polemicists of the 1920s had given extreme judgments on the *Confession:* total deceit, abject contrition. But must we view it as either a masterstroke or a tragic downfall? Bakunin himself invoked the title of Goethe's introspective autobiography to describe it as a mixture of *Dichtung* and *Wahrheit,* a blend of creative imagination and higher truth. Like Goethe, Bakunin was concerned not merely with the results of his life but with his life's symbolic meaning.

The frenzied years of revolutionary plotting, no less than the torture and daily interrogations of Saxon and Austrian jailers, were over. Bakunin was now alone, in a Russian prison; perhaps for the first time in his life a flood of memories burst forth, and he began to retrace his life and thoughts, searching for some higher meaning to compensate for the heartbreak of apparent failure. There is no need, as has been suggested, to credit Nicholas as a master technician craftily awaiting the proper psychological moment to send an affable Orlov to Bakunin's cell with a message of paternal concern.[39] Bakunin had tired physically since the beginning of his confinement because his biological nature, as he repeatedly said, demanded activity. Earlier in Russia and in Paris, during times of inactivity he had fallen into severe depression. Physically and emotionally Bakunin was ill equipped to endure confinement as well as did Chernyshevsky, for example, who was by nature introspective and capable of bearing solitude.

It is quite possible that when Orlov first visited him, Bakunin was eager to relate his past and thoughts to another human being, and certainly he knew that the tsar was the only person who could alter the fate he most dreaded—to rot for the remainder of his life within four walls. Bakunin did not hesitate; here was a challenge that awakened him from his stupor and torment. The tsar's invitation lifted his hopelessness and disclosed horizons Bakunin had thought no longer open to him. He would write to the tsar, who alone could mitigate his punishment. In the opinion of the émigré Russian scholar B. A. Evreinov (and apparently, as the first epigraph shows, of some persons at court), the challenge of writing to the tsar aroused in Bakunin the spirit of a clever gambler.[40] What had he to lose? He was alone, unsustained by even the consoling thought that the movement would continue without him, a belief that would comfort later generations of revolutionaries in Russia. Thus the critical task is not, as some writers have maintained, to discover what prompted Bakunin to write, but to untangle the many threads of aim and purpose interwoven in the *Confession*.

How did Bakunin hope to reach the despotic soul of Nicholas? What tone should he adopt? What attitude would best impress the tsar? How could he establish a common ground between them? Although Bakunin wrote in haste, there is every reason to presume that he carefully weighed his words. To deny his revolutionary activities and goals would have been foolish, since the Third Section possessed copious information obtained from its diplomatic representatives as well as from the Saxon and Austrian courts. Bakunin therefore would admit everything, accept full responsibility, and feign contrition in the hope of eliciting Nicholas' sympathy. Nevertheless, Bakunin the gambler sought more than the alleviation of his punishment; he sought communion with the tsar. By force of personality and argument he was accustomed to sway others to his views to serve his ends. The tsar, to be sure, was Bakunin's greatest challenge. Bakunin belabored the points upon which he believed autocrat and rebel agreed. His ridicule of German philosophy and German traits of character, his contempt for Western institutions, even his criticism of the Poles' inflated national vanity appealed to Nicholas' own prejudices and elicited emphatic concurrence in the tsar's marginal exclamations. But Bakunin's attempt to blame Russia's ills on the self-centered bureaucracy rather than on the sovereign himself did not draw a similar response. Bakunin's suggestion that Nicholas become the "people's tsar" and lead the Slavs against a decadent West provoked the tsar's categorical refusal to become a "Slav Masaniello."

Bakunin was occasionally inconsistent, however, in his aim of reaching the tsar. The *Confession* contains several passages, notably on the February Revolution in Paris, that, as Bakunin must have known, could only annoy Nicholas, and which were hardly necessary to maintain the mask of credibility. Was this simply defiance or was it involuntary resistance to the role he was playing? Was not the temptation too great to divulge to Nicholas "truths" that had never before penetrated the protective screen surrounding the Russian autocrat? [41]

Polonskii suggests that the *Confession* can be viewed as a competition between two obstinate players, a contest in which Bakunin was the loser.[42] Nicholas expected more than penitence and humility from his prisoner; he wanted facts, names, and specific information about conspiracies, especially of the Poles, directed against his person and the empire. In his very first marginal notation he rejected Bakunin's offer of a "conditional" confession—one that would not compromise others. This stance did not deter him from reading the proffered document with deep interest, almost excitement; perhaps he was even momentarily carried away by Bakunin's rhetoric. But Bakunin's gamble was foredoomed; the Russian bear was unreachable, as Bakunin later confided to Ralli.

At the conclusion of the *Confession*, Bakunin made two requests: to be transferred to forced labor and to be permitted a visit from his family. The latter was freely granted, but the former was denied. Bakunin's ploy had failed, and Nicholas left him to a "German punishment" for his "German sins." For one thing only was Bakunin grateful, he later wrote Herzen, and that was "for the fact that the tsar, receiving the Confession, did not interrogate me further about anything." [43]

Had not the Crimean War and Nicholas' death intervened, Bakunin might well have spent the rest of his life in prison. But in 1854, when it was feared that British and French ships might besiege St. Petersburg, Bakunin was transferred to the Schlüsselburg Fortress on the shore of nearby Lake Ladoga. After Alexander became tsar, Bakunin's family redoubled its efforts to obtain a commutation of his sentence, but his name was stricken from the list of those to be granted amnesty upon Alexander's accession. To Bakunin's mother, who implored the new tsar to reduce her son's punishment, Alexander purportedly replied, "Know, Madame, that as long as your son lives, he can never be free." [44]

Finally, on 14 February 1857, Mikhail himself petitioned the tsar for clemency.[45] This time there was no question of pretense; six years of imprisonment had undermined the spirit that had guided Bakunin's report to Nicholas. He begged Alexander to end his unbearable suffering. A week later Bakunin was offered the alternative of perpetual exile in Siberia, which he readily accepted.

Bakunin was to remain in Siberia only four years. In 1861 he left behind in Irkutsk the woman he had married, evaded the inept penal supervision, and made his way to the Pacific coast, where he found passage on a vessel to Japan. From there he reached San Francisco, then New York, and eventually he arrived in England. On the evening of 27 December 1861 he arrived at the London home of his old friend Alexander Herzen. It was fourteen years since they had parted in Paris on the eve of the 1848 revolution that would lead Bakunin on his long and ill-fated odyssey. His second exile was beginning. His Pan-Slavism discarded, he would become the prophet of revolutionary anarchism. His most fruitful years lay ahead, but the words he had written to Nicholas a decade before continued to haunt him.

The *Confession* is remarkable not only for the light it sheds on Bakunin's personality and on the Russia of Nicholas I; it is an invaluable, if not always reliable, account of the revolutionary generation of the 1840s and especially of the tumultuous years 1848–1849. Like the accounts of Herzen and Friedrich Engels that have long been available in English translation, the *Confession* reflects the mood of pessimism and recrimination that infected European intellectuals in the wake of the failure of the 1848 revolutionary struggles.[46] With Herzen, Bakunin despaired of Western parliamentary institutions and turned to his native Russia as the future mainspring of humanity's regeneration. The brief gathering of Slavs in Prague, which emerges as the high point of his first exile, kindled Bakunin's faith in the revolutionary potential of the Slav peoples. Although Bakunin and Engels stand together in their call for dismantling the Habsburg Empire, Bakunin's Germanophobia—a principal leitmotif of the *Confession*—clashes sharply with Engels' indictment of the "unhistorical" Habsburg Slavs, especially the Czechs and the Croats, as servants of the counterrevolutionary court camarilla. Yet in May 1849, when Bakunin was offered the cause of revolution, he chose neither the Slavs nor the Germans. He stayed in Dresden to fight for a cause he knew was hopeless, motivated by the same feelings that had led him to embrace the similarly ill-fated uprising in Prague a year earlier.

The *Confession* reflects Bakunin's political maturation in the midst of the burgeoning political and social currents of the 1840s and the storm of conflicting political and national aspirations spawned by the revolutions of 1848. But as a psychological document, the *Confession* defies facile classification. It portrays a man disillusioned by the failure of his political hopes and tormented by solitary confinement, and at the same time an individual of keen imagination and undaunted spirit.

CONFESSION

Mikhail Bakunin

[July–August 1851;
Peter and Paul Fortress,
St. Petersburg]

Your Imperial Majesty,
Most Gracious Sovereign!

When I was being conveyed from Austria to Russia, knowing the severity of Russian laws, knowing YOUR insuperable hatred for everything that even resembles disobedience, to say nothing of open rebellion against the will of YOUR IMPERIAL MAJESTY,* also knowing all the gravity of my crimes, which I had neither hope nor even the intention of hiding or minimizing before the court, I told myself that only one thing remained for me: *to suffer to the end;* and I prayed God for the strength to drink, in a worthy manner and without base weakness, the bitter cup that I myself had prepared. I knew that, having been deprived several years ago of my gentry status by verdict of the Governing Senate and by ukase of Your Imperial Majesty, I could be legally subjected to corporal punishment, and, expecting the worst, I hoped only for death, as a swift deliverer from all torments and from all ordeals.

I cannot express, Sire, how I was struck, deeply touched by the noble, humane, indulgent treatment that greeted me immediately upon crossing the Russian border! I expected a different reception. What I saw, heard, everything I experienced in the course of the entire journey, from the Kingdom of Poland to the Peter and Paul Fortress, was so contrary to my fear-

On the first page of the manuscript Nicholas wrote to his son, later Alexander II: "You should read this through, it's very interesting and instructive."

* Following the custom of tsarist Russia, words such as "Sire," "Your Majesty," and so on, referring to the tsar, were written in capital letters. Hereafter, only the initial capitals of such words will be used.

ful expectations, stood in such contradiction to all that I myself, on the basis of rumors, had thought and spoken and written about the brutality of the Russian government, that I, for the first time doubting the truth of my former ideas, asked myself with amazement: Did I not commit slander? A sojourn of two months in the Peter and Paul Fortress finally convinced me of the complete baselessness of many of my old prejudices.

Do not think, however, Sire, that I, encouraged by such humane treatment, came to have any false or vain hope. I understand very well that severity of laws does not rule out love for mankind, just as, conversely, love for mankind does not rule out severe execution of the laws. I know how great are my crimes and, having lost the right to hope, I hope for nothing; and if I am to tell you the truth, Sire, I have so aged and become so heavy of heart in recent years that I hardly wish for anything at all.

Count Orlov has informed me on behalf of Your Imperial Majesty that you wish, Sire, that I write for you a complete confession of all my transgressions.[1] Sire! I do not deserve such grace, and I blush remembering all that I dared say and write concerning the implacable severity of Your Imperial Majesty.

How shall I write? What shall I say to the terrible Russian Tsar, to the dread Guardian and zealous Upholder of the laws? My confession to you, as my sovereign, would consist of the following few words: Sire! I am entirely guilty before Your Imperial Majesty and before the laws of the fatherland. You know my crimes, and what is known to you is sufficient to condemn me, according to the laws, to the harshest punishment existing in Russia. I was in open revolt against you, Sire, and against your government; I dared oppose you as an enemy; I wrote, spoke, incited minds against you wherever and as much as I could. What more is needed? Command that I be judged and punished, Sire; and your judgment and your punishment will be lawful and just. What more could I write to my sovereign? *

But Count Orlov, on behalf of Your Imperial Majesty, spoke

* The vertical lines in the margins of the manuscript were made by Nicholas.

to me words that shook me to the depths of my soul and turned my whole heart: "Write," he said to me, "write to the sovereign as though you were speaking with your spiritual father."

Yes, Sire, I shall confess to you as to a spiritual father from whom a man expects forgiveness, not here but for the other world; and I pray God that He inspire in me words that are simple, sincere, heartfelt, without contrivance or adulation; in a word, worthy of finding access to the heart of Your Imperial Majesty.

I implore you for only two things, Sire! First, do not doubt the truth of my words; I swear to you that no lie, not the thousandth part of a lie, shall flow from my pen. And second, I implore you, Sire, DO NOT DEMAND THAT I CONFESS TO YOU THE SINS OF OTHERS. FOR IN GOOD CONSCIENCE NO ONE CAN BARE THE SINS OF OTHERS, ONLY HIS OWN.* From the complete shipwreck that has befallen me, I have saved only one good: my honor and the consciousness that for my salvation and the alleviation of my lot, never, either in Saxony or in Austria, was I a traitor. And the repugnant realization that I had betrayed someone's trust, or even had revealed a word carelessly spoken in my presence, would be more agonizing to me than torture itself. And in your own eyes, Sire, I would rather be a criminal deserving of the most cruel punishment than be a scoundrel.

And so I shall begin my confession.

In order that it be complete, I must say several words concerning my early youth. I studied for three years in the Artillery School, was promoted to officer's rank at the age of nineteen, and at the end of the fourth [year] of my training, being in the first officers' class, I fell in love, became bewildered, ceased studying, passed my examination in the most shameful manner or, to say it better, did not pass it at all, and for this was sent to serve in Lithuania with the condition that

* Words in small capitals were underscored by Nicholas. Note by Nicholas in margin here: "Precisely by this he destroys all confidence: if he feels all the weight of his sins, then only a PURE, complete confession, and not a CONDITIONAL one, can be considered a confession."

for three years I would be passed over for promotion and that until I reached the rank of second lieutenant I would not be permitted to retire or go on leave. In this manner my career in the service was ruined at the very beginning through my own fault and in spite of the truly paternal concern shown me by Mikhail Mikhailovich Kovan'ko, who was then commander of the Artillery School.[2]

Having served one year in Lithuania, with great difficulty I went on the retired list, wholly against my father's wish. After I left military service, I learned German and threw myself avidly into the study of German philosophy, from which I expected light and salvation. Blessed with a fervid imagination and, as the French say, *d'une grande dose d'exaltation* *—forgive me, Sire, I cannot find the Russian expression—I caused my old father much sorrow, for which, although it is late, I now repent with all my soul. I can say only one thing in my justification: My follies then, as well as my later sins and crimes, were alien to all base, selfish motives; they sprang in large part from false concepts, but even more from a powerful and never satisfied need for knowledge, life, and action.

In the year 1840, the twenty-seventh from my birth, with difficulty I obtained permission from my father to go abroad to pursue a course in sciences at the University of Berlin. I studied for a year and a half in Berlin. In the first year of my stay abroad and in the beginning of the second I was still a stranger, just as I had formerly been in Russia, to all political problems, which I even disdained, looking at them from the heights of philosophic abstraction. My indifference to them went so far that I did not even want to take a newspaper in my hands. I studied the sciences, especially German metaphysics, in which I was exclusively immersed almost to the point of insanity, seeing nothing day and night besides Hegel's categories. Germany itself cured me of the philosophical disease that prevailed in that country, however; becoming more closely acquainted with metaphysical problems, I became convinced rather quickly of the insignificance and vanity of all metaphysics; I searched in it for life but in it is death and te-

* With a great deal of excitement.

dium; I searched for a cause but in it is absolute emptiness. This discovery was facilitated not a little by my personal acquaintance with German professors, for what now can be more pitiful, funnier, than a German professor or even a German in general! He who gets to know German life intimately cannot like German science; and German philosophy is a clear product of German life and occupies the same place among the real sciences that the Germans themselves occupy among the living nations. At last it became repulsive to me and I ceased studying it. Being cured of German metaphysics in this manner, I was not, however, cured of a thirst for the new, of the desire and hope of searching out for myself in Western Europe a noble subject for study and a broad field for action. The unhappy thought of not returning to Russia had already begun to glimmer in my mind. I abandoned philosophy and threw myself into politics.

Finding myself in this transitional state, I moved from Berlin to Dresden; I began to read political journals. With the accession to the throne of the presently reigning Prussian King,[3] Germany took a new direction: through his speeches, promises, innovations, the King agitated, set in motion not only Prussia but all the other German lands, so that Dr. Ruge [4] not without basis nicknamed him the first German revolutionary—forgive me, Sire, for expressing myself so boldly in speaking of a crowned personage. At this time there appeared in Germany a large number of brochures, journals, political verses, and I read them all avidly. At this same time one first heard talk of communism; Dr. Stein's book *Die Socialisten in Frankreich* [5] appeared and produced almost as strong and general an impression as Dr. Strauss's *Das Leben Jesu* [6] had earlier, and opened for me a new world into which I threw myself with all the fervor of one who hungers and thirsts. It seemed to me that I was hearing the proclamation of a new dispensation, the revelation of a new religion of exaltation, dignity, happiness, liberation of the entire human race. I began to read the works of the French democrats and socialists, and devoured all that I could get hold of in Dresden. I soon became acquainted with Dr. Arnold Ruge, who was then publishing

Die Deutsche Jahrbücher, a journal that was then in almost the same transition from philosophy to politics. I wrote for him a philosophically revolutionary article entitled "Die Parteien in Deutschland" under the pseudonym of Jules Elysard.[7] And so ill fated and heavy was my hand from the very start that no sooner did the article appear than the journal itself was banned. This was at the end of 1842.

Then the political poet Georg Herwegh arrived in Dresden from Switzerland.[8] All Germany was making a fuss over him, and he was received with honor by the Prussian King himself, who soon thereafter expelled the poet from his domains. Leaving aside Herwegh's political orientation, about which I dare not speak before Your Imperial Majesty, I must say that he is a pure, truly noble man with a generous soul, such as is seldom found in a German—a man seeking the truth and not his own profit or advantage. I made his acquaintance, became friendly with him, and remained on amicable terms with him to the end. The above-mentioned article in the *Deutsche Jahrbücher,* my acquaintance with Ruge and his circle, and especially my friendly relationship with Herwegh, who openly called himself a republican, a relationship, however, that was not political although it was based on a similarity of thoughts, needs, and tendencies—not political because it did not have any decidedly positive goal—all this turned the attention of the embassy in Dresden to me. I heard that they had supposedly begun to speak of the necessity of returning me to Russia; but returning to Russia seemed death to me! In Western Europe an endless horizon was opening before me, I yearned for life, miracles, wide freedom; but in Russia I saw darkness, spiritual coldness, torpor, inertia—and I decided to break with my motherland. All my subsequent sins and misfortunes resulted from this thoughtless step. Herwegh was obliged to leave Germany; I set out with him for Switzerland—if he had gone to America I would have gone even there with him—and settled in Zurich in January 1843.

Just as I had gradually begun to recover from my philosophical illness in Berlin, so my political disillusionment started in Switzerland. But since a political infirmity is more

severe, more harmful, and more deeply embedded in the soul
than a philosophical one, so for its cure there was required
more time, more bitter experiences; IT BROUGHT ME TO THAT
UNENVIABLE SITUATION IN WHICH I NOW FIND MYSELF, AND
EVEN NOW I DO NOT KNOW WHETHER I HAVE ENTIRELY RECOV-
ERED FROM IT.* I dare not take up the time of Your Imperial
Majesty with a description of internal Swiss politics; in my
opinion it can be expressed in two words: dirty gossip. The
greater part of the Swiss journals are in the hands of German
immigrants—I am speaking here only of German Switzerland—and Germans in general are so devoid of social tact
that any polemic in their hands is usually turned into a dirty
fight in which there is no end of petty and vile personal slander.

In Zurich I became acquainted with Herwegh's acquaintances and friends, whom I liked so little, however, that during
the course of the whole time I spent in that city I avoided
frequent meetings with them and was in close contact only
with Herwegh. At that time the Zurich republic was ruled by
Councilor of State Bluntschli, the head of the conservative
party. His journal, *Der Schweizerische Beobachter*, carried on a
savage struggle with the organ of the democratic party, *Der
Schweizerische Republikaner*, published by Julius Fröbel, an acquaintance and even friend of Herwegh.[9] Neither do I dare
speak of the subject of their quarrel at that time: there is too
much filth in it. It was not a purely political quarrel such as
sometimes takes place between warring parties in other states;
even religious charlatans, prophets, and messiahs took part in
it, together with noble freeloading knights, simply thieves,
and even indecent women, who later sat in the dock with Mr.
Bluntschli as witnesses and defendants in the public trial that
ended this scandalous battle. Bluntschli and his friends the
Rhomer brothers, one calling himself the messiah and the
other a prophet, were convicted and put to shame, together
with these ladies.[10] The democrats triumphed, although they
themselves came out of this shameful business not without
shame; and Bluntschli, in order to take revenge upon them—

* Nicholas' marginal note: "NB."

and probably also in obedience to a demand of the Prussian government—banished the completely innocent Herwegh from Zurich canton.

As for me, I lived apart from all these squabbles, seldom seeing anyone but Herwegh. I was not acquainted either with Mr. Bluntschli or with his friends; I read, studied, and thought of means by which I might honorably gain a living, for I no longer received money from home. But Bluntschli, probably learning of my friendly connection with Herwegh—What is not known in a small city!—and perhaps in order to curry favor with the Russian government, wanted to embroil me too, and toward this end the following convenient occasion soon presented itself.

Herwegh, who was already in Aargau canton, sent to me, with a note of recommendation, the communist tailor Weitling, who, traveling from Lausanne to Zurich, had stopped by on the way to make his acquaintance.[11] Now Herwegh, knowing how social problems interested me then, recommended him to me. I was glad of this opportunity to learn—from a living source—about communism, which was then already beginning to attract general attention. I liked Weitling; he is an uneducated man, but I found in him much natural keen-wittedness, a quick mind, much energy, and especially much wild fanaticism, noble pride, and faith in the liberation and future of the enslaved majority. He did not retain these qualities for long, however, becoming spoiled soon after in the company of communist men of letters; but at the time he was very much to my liking. I was so satiated by the saccharine conversation of petty German professors and literary men that I was glad to meet a man who was fresh, simple, and uneducated, but energetic and believing. I asked him to visit me; he came to my place rather often, expounding his theory to me and telling me much about the French communists, about the life of workers in general, about their labors, hopes, amusements, and also about the German communist societies that had just been started. I argued against his theory, but listened to his facts with great curiosity; my relations with Weitling were limited to this. I had positively no other connection with him or with other communists at that time or later, and I myself was never a communist.

I shall stop here, Sire, and shall go somewhat deeper into this subject, knowing that more than once I have been accused before the government of active association with communists, first by Mr. Bluntschli, then probably by others also. I want to clear myself once and for all of unjust accusations; there are already so many, so many heavy sins on me, then why should I take upon myself still other sins of which I definitely was not guilty?

Subsequently I knew many French, German, Belgian, and English socialists and communists, read their works, studied their theories, but I never belonged to any sect or to any society and definitely remained apart from their undertakings, their propaganda and activities. I followed with constant interest the movement of socialism, and especially of communism, for I looked upon it as a natural, necessary, inevitable result of the economic and political development of Western Europe; * I saw in it a young, elemental force not yet knowing its power, which has been summoned either to renew or completely destroy the western states. The social order, social organization have rotted in the West and barely maintain themselves through painful effort; by this alone are explained that unbelievable weakness and that panic terror which in 1848 overtook all the states in the West, excluding England; but she too, apparently, will be overtaken in a short time by that same fate. In Western Europe, no matter where you turn, everywhere you see decrepitude, weakness, unbelief, and depravity, the depravity that comes from unbelief; beginning with the very top of the social ladder, not a single person, not a single privileged class has faith in its calling and rights; all play the charlatan one toward the other, and not one trusts any other that is beneath it: privileges, classes, and governments are barely maintained through egotism and habit †—a weak impediment

* Bakunin's note: "I am speaking only of Western Europe because neither in the East nor in any Slavic land—with the possible exception of Bohemia and in part Moravia and Silesia—did communism have a place or make sense."

† Nicholas' marginal note: "A striking truth."

to the growing storm! Culture has become equated with depravity of mind and heart, equated with impotence—and in
the midst of all this general rotting only the rude, unenlight-
ened people, called the mob, has preserved in itself freshness
and power, not in Germany, however, as in France. Moreover,
all reasoning and arguments that first served the aristocracy
against the monarchy, and then the middle class against the
monarchy and the aristocracy, now serve—and almost with
more power—the popular masses against the monarchy, the
aristocracy, and the petty bourgeoisie. In this, in my opinion,
is the essence and the power of communism—to say nothing
of the growing poverty of the working class—the natural consequence of the increase of the proletariat, an increase that in
turn is necessarily connected with the development of factory
industry such as that which exists in the West. Communism
proceeded and proceeds at least as much from above as from
below; below, among the popular masses, it grows and lives
as an unclear yet energetic necessity, as an instinct to elevate
oneself; among the upper classes as depravity, as egotism, as
an instinct of menacing, deserved misfortune, as a vague and
helpless terror resulting from decrepitude and an unclean conscience; and this terror and the incessant outcry against communism facilitated its spread almost more than did the communists' propaganda itself.* It seems to me that this vague,
invisible, impalpable but ubiquitous communism, which lives
in one form or another in everyone without exception, is a
thousand times more dangerous than that which is defined
and systematized, which is preached only in a few organized,
secret or open communist societies.† The impotence of these
last was obviously demonstrated in 1848 in England, France,
Belgium, and especially Germany; and there is nothing easier
than to search out absurdity, contradictions, and impossibilities in every social theory known to this date, so that not

---

* Bakunin's note: "Bluntschli's brochure, for example, which was published
in 1843 in the name of the Zurich government on the occasion of Weitling's
trial, was, together with the aforementioned book by Stein, one of the principal causes for the spread of communism in Germany."
† Nicholas' marginal note: "True!"

even one is in a condition to survive even three days of existence.

Forgive, Sire, this brief discourse; but my transgressions are so closely tied to my sinful thoughts that I absolutely cannot confess the one without mentioning the other. I was obliged to show why I could not have belonged to any sect of socialists or communists, as I have been unjustly accused of doing. While understanding the reason for the existence of these sects, I did not like their theories; not sharing the latter, I could not be an instrument of their propaganda; and finally, I also valued my independence too highly to agree to be the slave and blind tool of any secret society at all, to say nothing of one whose opinions I could not share. At this very time, that is in 1843, communism in Switzerland consisted of a small number of German workers; in Lausanne and Geneva openly, as societies for singing, reading, and common work; in Zurich, on the other hand, it consisted of five or six tailors and cobblers. Among the Swiss there were no communists: the nature of the Swiss is adverse to any kind of communism, and German communism was then still in swaddling clothes. But in order to make himself important in the eyes of the rulers of Europe, and in part in the vain hope of compromising the Zurich radicals, Bluntschli set up a fantastic scarecrow. By his own admission he knew of Weitling's arrival in Zurich, tolerated his presence for two or three months, and then ordered him seized, hoping to find among his papers enough important documents to embarrass the Zurich radicals. But he found nothing except some stupid correspondence and gossip.* And against me, two or three of Weitling's letters in which he speaks a few insignificant words concerning me, informing his friend in one of them that he had become acquainted with a Russian,

* Bakunin's note: "As proof that all Mr. Bluntschli's accusations, conclusions, and guesses and the entire structure based upon them were vain and false, I shall cite only one fact: Weitling was sentenced by the Supreme Court to one or two years in prison, and not for communism but for a stupid book that he had printed in Zurich not long before. Immediately after the sentence was pronounced, Bluntschli did not imprison Weitling but handed him over to the Prussian government, which, having reviewed the case, set Weitling free a month later." [12]

and calling me by name; whereas in another he calls me *der Russe,* adding that *der Russe ist ein guter* or *ein prächtiger Kerl,** and so forth. This is what Mr. Bluntschli's accusations against me were based upon; there could be no other basis, for my acquaintance with Weitling was limited only to curiosity on my part and to a desire to confide on his; and except for Weitling I did not know a single communist in Zurich. Hearing, however—and I do not know if this rumor was true or not—that Bluntschli even intended to arrest me, and fearing the consequences, I left Zurich. I lived several months in the small town of Nyon on the shore of Lake Geneva in complete isolation, struggling with destitution. And then I lived in Bern, where in January or February of 1844 I learned from Mr. Struve, the secretary of the embassy in Switzerland, that the embassy, having received a denunciation of me from Bluntschli, wrote to Petersburg about it and was awaiting instructions. In this denunciation, according to Mr. Struve's tale, Bluntschli, not satisfied with accusing me of communism, asserted—again falsely—that I was writing or preparing to write a book about Russia and Poland directed against the Russian government. [13]

There was at least a shade of plausibility in accusing me of communism: my acquaintance with Weitling. But this latest accusation was definitely devoid of any basis and clearly proved to me Bluntschli's evil intent; for not only had I not yet thought of writing or printing anything about Russia, but I tried not even to think of her because the memory of her tormented me; and my mind was directed exclusively toward Western Europe. As far as Poland is concerned, I can say that at that time I did not even remember her existence. In Berlin I avoided acquaintance with Poles and saw some of them only at the university. In Dresden and Switzerland I did not see a single Pole. [14]

In 1844, Sire, my sins were internal, mental sins, and not sins in deed: I ate not one but many fruits of the forbidden tree of the knowledge of good and evil—a great sin, the source

---

* "The Russian is a good" or "a fine fellow."

and beginning of all subsequent crimes, but as yet not taking the form of any action or any intention. In my thoughts and inclination I was already a complete and arrant democrat, but in life I was inexperienced, stupid, and almost as innocent as a child. In refusing to go to Russia in response to the command of the government, I committed my first actual crime.

Consequently, I quit Switzerland and set out for Belgium in the company of my friend Reichel.[15] I must say several words about him; his name is mentioned rather often in the documents of indictment. Adolph Reichel, Prussian citizen, composer and pianist, is alien to all politics, and if he has even heard of politics it must only have been through me. Having become acquainted in Dresden and meeting again later in Switzerland, we were drawn to each other and became friends. He was always my true and only friend. I lived with him inseparably, sometimes even at his expense, right down to 1848. When I was forced to leave Switzerland, he, not wishing to leave me, traveled with me to Belgium.

In Brussels I became acquainted with Lelewel.[16] Here for the first time my thoughts turned toward Russia and Poland. Being an absolute democrat at the time, I began to look at them through the eyes of a democrat, although still unclearly and in a very ill-defined manner. National feeling, awakening in me after a long sleep as a result of friction with Polish national feeling, came into conflict with my democratic concepts and conclusions. I saw Lelewel often, asked many things about the Polish revolution, the intentions of the Poles, their plans in case of victory, and their hopes for the future. And I argued with him more than once, especially about Little Russia [17] and Belorussia, both of which, according to Polish views, should have belonged to Poland; whereas according to mine, they—especially Little Russia—should have hated Poland as their ancient oppressor. Of all the Poles then in Brussels, however, I knew and saw only Lelewel, and although we saw each other often, my relations with him never went beyond the bounds of ordinary acquaintance. True, I was going to translate into Russian that *Manifesto to the Russians* for which he was expelled from Paris, but this was without consequence: the translation remained unpublished among my papers.[18]

Having spent several months in Brussels, I set out with Reichel for Paris, from which, just as earlier in Berlin and then in Switzerland, I now expected salvation and light. This was in July of 1844.[19]

From the start Paris acted on me like a tub of cold water on a feverish man. Nowhere had I ever felt so alone, so alienated, so disoriented—forgive the expression, Sire—as in Paris. My acquaintances at first were almost exclusively German democrats who either were exiled or had come voluntarily from Germany in order to found here a democratic Franco-German journal with the goal of bringing into accord and association the spiritual and political interests of both peoples.[20] But since German men of letters cannot live with one another without quarrels, profanity, and gossip, the whole undertaking, announced with such great noise, vanished into thin air, ending with the unfortunate and foul weekly sheet *Vorwärts*, which also did not last long but soon sank in its own filth. And the Germans themselves were soon driven from Paris, to my not inconsiderable relief.[21]

At that time—that is, at the end of autumn 1844—I first heard of the sentence condemning me and Ivan Golovin to deprivation of gentry status and to penal servitude. I did not hear this officially but from an acquaintance—it seems to me it was from Golovin himself. On this occasion he wrote an article in the *Gazette des tribunaux* on the imaginary rights of the Russian aristocracy, which had supposedly been outraged and trampled upon in our persons.[22] In answer to him and in refutation, I wrote another article in the democratic journal *Réforme* in the form of a letter to the editor. This letter—the first word of mine concerning Russia to appear in print—was my second actual crime. It appeared in the journal *Réforme* with my signature at the end of 1844—I don't remember which month—and is doubtless in the hands of the government among the documents of indictment.[23]

After my departure from Brussels I did not see a single Pole until this very time. My article in *Réforme* was the occasion for my new acquaintance with some of them. In the first place, Prince Adam Czartoryski, through one of his followers, invited me to his home.[24] I was at his home once, but after this I never saw him again. Subsequently I received from London a congratulatory letter with compliments from the Polish democrats and an invitation to the ceremony of mourning held by them every year in memory of Ryleev, Pestel, and others.[25] I answered them with similar compliments, thanked them for their fraternal sympathy, but did not go to London, for I had not yet determined in my own mind the relationship in which I—though a democrat, a Russian all the same—should stand toward the Polish emigration and toward the Western public in general. I still feared noisy, empty, and useless demonstrations and phrases, for which I was never a great enthusiast. Thus ended for the time being my relations with the Poles, and until the spring of 1846 I did not see a single one with the exception of Alojzy Biernacki (who held the post of minister of finance during the Polish revolution), a kind, venerable old man with whom I had become acquainted at the home of Nikolai Ivanovich Turgenev.[26] Living far from all political parties of the emigration, Biernacki was occupied exclusively with his Polish school. I also sometimes saw Mickiewicz, whom I had respected in the past as a great Slav poet but whom I now pitied as a half-deceived, half-deceiving apostle and prophet of a new absurd religion and of a new messiah.[27] Mickiewicz tried to convert me because in his opinion if one Pole, one Russian, one Czech, one Frenchman, and one Jew agreed to live and act together in the spirit of Towiański, it is enough to overturn and save the world.[28] He had enough Poles and there were some Czechs; there were also Jews and Frenchmen. All that was lacking was a Russian; he wanted to recruit me but could not.

Among Frenchmen I had the following acquaintances. From the constitutional party: Chambolle, editor [*rédacteur*] of *Le Siècle*; Merruau, managing editor [*gérant*] of *Le Constitutionnel*;

Emile Girardin, editor of *La Presse;* Durrieu, editor of *Le Courrier français;* the economists Léon Faucher, Frédéric Bastiat and Wolowski, and others. From the party of political republicans: Béranger, Lamennais, François, Etienne, and Emmanuel Arago, and the editors of *Le National,* Marrast and Bastide. From the party of democrats: the deceased Cavaignac, brother of the general; Flocon and Louis Blanc, editors of *La Réforme;* Victor Considérant, *fouriériste* * and editor of *La Démocratie pacifique;* Pascal Duprat, editor of the *Revue indépendante;* Félix Pyat, the negrophile Victor Schoelcher; the professors Michelet and Quinet; Proudhon the utopian, and despite this without any doubt one of the most remarkable contemporary Frenchmen; finally, George Sand and a few other less well-known ones.[29] I saw some less often, others more often, not having close relations with a single one. Several times at the very beginning of my stay in Paris I also visited some French *ouvriers* †—a society of communists and socialists—with no motive or aim other than curiosity. But I soon ceased going to them, in the first place in order not to attract the attention of the French government and bring on myself unwarranted persecution, but mainly because I found that visiting these societies was not of the slightest benefit to me. Most often of all I saw—not speaking of Reichel, with whom I lived inseparably—most often I saw my old friend Herwegh, who had also moved to Paris and who was concerned at that time almost exclusively with natural sciences, and Nikolai Ivanovich Turgenev. The latter lived with his family, far from all political movement and, one might say, from any society, and, at least as far as I was able to note, wished for nothing so passionately as for forgiveness and permission to return to Russia to live out his last years in his motherland, which he remembered with love and not infrequently with tears. At his home I sometimes met the Italian Count Mamiani, who was later papal minister in Rome, and the Neapolitan General Pepe.[30]

* A follower of François Marie Charles Fourier (1772–1837), who advocated the reorganization of society into small socialist communes.
† Workers.

I also sometimes saw Russians who had come to Paris. But I implore you, Sire, DO NOT DEMAND NAMES OF ME. Only I assure you—and remember, Sire, at the beginning of this epistle I swore to you * that not a single lie, not even one thousandth part of a lie would defile the purity of my sincere confession—and now I swear to you that neither then nor later did I have any political relations with a single Russian, nor did I have even a shadow of a political connection with a single one, either face to face or through a third party or by correspondence. The Russian newcomers and I lived in completely different spheres: they lived as the wealthy live—gaily, giving banquets, luncheons, and dinners to one another; they debauched, drank, went to theaters and balls *avec grisettes et lorettes* †—a way of life for which I had not the slightest inclination, much less means. For I was living in poverty, painfully struggling with circumstances and with my inner, never satisfied needs for life and action, and I never shared their amusements, their labors, or their pursuits. I DO NOT SAY THAT I NEVER TRIED—AND ESPECIALLY BEGINNING IN 1846—TO CONVERT SOME OF THEM TO MY THINKING AND TO WHAT I THEN CALLED AND CONSIDERED A GOOD CAUSE. BUT NOT A SINGLE EFFORT OF MINE WAS SUCCESSFUL. THEY LISTENED TO ME WITH SMILES, CALLED ME AN ECCENTRIC, SO THAT AFTER SEVERAL VAIN ATTEMPTS I REFRAINED ENTIRELY FROM ASSOCIATING WITH THEM. THE ENTIRE GUILT OF SOME OF THEM CONSISTED IN THIS: THAT SEEING MY MISERY THEY SOMETIMES—AND VERY RARELY AT THAT—HELPED ME.‡

I lived at home for the most part, spending some of my time in translating from the German in order to earn a living, and some in the sciences: history, statistics, political economy, socioeconomic systems, speculative politics (i.e., politics with no application whatsoever). I also spent some time with mathematics and the natural sciences. Here I must make one observation in defense of my own honor: Parisian booksellers, and

---

* Nicholas' marginal note: "NB" (according to Polonskii; not in Steklov).
† With shopgirls and tarts.
‡ Nicholas' marginal note: "NB."

German ones too, frequently tried to persuade me to write about Russia, offering me rather favorable terms. But I always refused, not wanting to make Russia the object of a commercial literary deal. I never wrote about Russia for money and not otherwise *qu'à mon corps défendant* *—I might say, reluctantly, almost against my will, and always under my own name. Except for the aforementioned article in the *Réforme* and another article in the *Constitutionnel,* and that unfortunate speech for which I was expelled from Paris, [31] I printed not one word about Russia. I am not speaking here of what I wrote after February 1848, when I was engaged in definite political activity. Even then, however, my publications were limited to two appeals and some articles in journals.

It was difficult, very difficult for me to live in Paris, Sire! Not so much because of poverty, which I bore with considerable equanimity, as because, having finally awakened from my youthful delirium and my fantastic youthful expectations, I suddenly found myself in an alien land, in a cold moral atmosphere, without relatives, without a family, without a round of activities, without a job, and with no hope for a better future. Having cut myself off from my native land and having thoughtlessly barred all paths to my return, I could not become either a German or a Frenchman. On the contrary, the longer I lived abroad, the more deeply I felt that I was a Russian and that I would never cease being a Russian. I could not return to Russian life except by a criminal revolutionary path in which I had little trust then, and which, if I am to tell the truth, I subsequently trusted only by painful, supernatural effort and by violently stifling an inner voice that whispered to me ceaselessly of the absurdity of my hopes and undertakings. Sometimes it was so difficult for me that more than once, in the evening, I stopped on the bridge over which I usually came home, asking myself if I would not do better to throw myself into the Seine and drown in it my joyless and useless existence.

Moreover, at this time the whole world was plunged in a grave lethargy. After the brief turmoil that occurred in Ger-

* Except in self-defense.

many upon the accession to the Prussian throne of the presently reigning King, and after the ephemeral movement produced several months later in all Europe by the Eastern Question, during the brief ministry of Thiers, [32] it seemed that the world had fallen asleep, and had fallen into such a deep sleep that no one, not even the most eccentric democrats, believed that it would soon awake. At the time no one yet saw that this was the calm before the storm. Now the French, as is known, were postponing all their hopes until the death of the late King Louis-Philippe. [33] It is true that as early as the end of 1844 Marrast once said to me: "La révolution est imminente, mais on ne peut jamais prédire quand et comment se fera une révolution française; la France est comme ce chaudron à vapeur, toujours prêt à éclater et dont nul ne sait prévoir l'explosion." * But both Marrast and his friends and, in general, all democrats were then still going about crestfallen and in the deepest dejection. But the conservative party exulted, promising itself life everlasting. And the public, from boredom, devoted itself to scandalous electoral and Jesuitical goings-on and even to the overseas movement of the English free-traders.†

In mid-1845, after a long calm, there were seen—not by everyone, but only by those following German developments—there were seen, I say, the first weak waves on the political ocean: in Germany there appeared two new religious sects, *die Lichtfreunde und die Deutschkatholiken.*‡ [34] In France some laughed at them, whereas others saw in them—and it seems to me not without foundation—signs of the times, portents of the weather. These sects, insignificant in themselves, were important in that they translated modern concepts and aspirations into religious language; i.e., into the language of the people. They could not have great influence on the educated classes, but they did act on the imagination of the

---

* "The revolution is imminent, but one can never predict when and how a French revolution will come about; France is like that steam boiler, always ready to burst and whose explosion no one can foresee."
† Bakunin uses the English expression "free-traders."
‡ The Friends of Light and the German Catholics.

masses, who are always more inclined toward religious fanaticism. Moreover, German Catholicism was invented and loosed upon the world (with a purely political goal) as the democratic party in Prussian Silesia. It was more effective than its older Protestant sister, which in turn was more honorable; among its apostles and propagators were many unsavory charlatans, but also many gifted people, and one may say that under the guise of general participation in communion—allegedly revived from the time of the original church—German Catholicism obviously preached communism.

But all the interest aroused by the appearance of these sects evaporated when the rumor arose that King Frederick William IV had given his state a constitution. Germany became agitated again, and it was as though France were rising for the first time from its deep slumber. There followed rapidly, like one thunder clap after another, first the Polish movement, then the events in Switzerland and Italy, and finally the revolution of 1848. I shall dwell on the Polish uprising because it constitutes an epoch in my own life.

Before 1846 I was alien to all political undertakings. I was not acquainted with the Polish democrats; it seemed the Germans were definitely not undertaking anything at that time; and the Frenchmen with whom I was acquainted told me nothing. Having long had close ties with the Polish democrats, they knew without a doubt of the Polish uprising that was being readied. But Frenchmen know how to keep a secret, and since my relations with them were limited to simple, superficial acquaintance, I could find out nothing from them. So the Poznań schemes, the venture in the Kingdom of Poland, the Kraków uprising, and the events in Galicia startled me at least as much as they did all the rest of the public.[35] The impression they made in Paris was incredible: for two or three days the whole population lived on the streets; stranger spoke with stranger, everyone asked for news, and all awaited reports from Poland with anxious impatience. This sudden awakening, this common movement of passions and minds, also seized me with its waves. It was as though I had awakened— and I decided that come what might, I would break out of my inaction and undertake active participation in the events that were about to occur.

For this I had to attract once more the attention of the Poles, who had already succeeded in forgetting about me. With this aim I wrote an article on Poland and the Belorussian Uniates, about which all the western European journals were then writing. This article, which appeared in the *Constitutionnel* early in the spring of 1846, is doubtless in the hands of the government.[36] When I gave it to Merruau, managing editor of *Le Constitutionnel*, he said to me: "Qu'on mette le feu aux quatre coins du monde pourvu que nous sortions de cet état honteux et insupportable!" * I reminded him of these words in February of 1848, but by then he had already repented, frightened just as were all the other liberals of the dynastic opposition by this terrible and at the same time strange revolution that they themselves had courted.

Before 1846 my sins were not intentional sins but rather were unthinking and, one might say, youthful. Having become a man in years, I still remained for long an inexperienced youth. From this time I began to sin consciously, intentionally, and with a more or less definite goal. Sire! I shall not attempt to excuse my inexcusable crimes, nor shall I speak to you of my later REPENTANCE—REPENTANCE IN MY SITUATION IS JUST AS USELESS AS THE REPENTANCE OF A SINNER AFTER DEATH—BUT I SHALL SIMPLY RELATE THE FACTS AND SHALL NOT CONCEAL OR MINIMIZE A SINGLE ONE.†

Soon after the appearance of the aforesaid article I set out for Versailles, without any summons, of my own volition, in order to become acquainted with and, if possible, draw close to and make common cause with the Centralizacja of the Polish Democratic Society, which was there at that time.[37] I wanted to propose to them joint action concerning the Russians living in the Kingdom of Poland, in Lithuania, and in Podolia, supposing that they had connections in these prov-

---

* "Let the four corners of the earth be set afire, just so we get out of this shameful and unbearable state!"

† Nicholas' marginal note: "Not true! The repentance of any sinner—if sincere—can bring salvation."

inces sufficient for active and successful propaganda. The goal I set was a Russian revolution and a republican federation of all the Slav lands—the basis of a unified and indivisible Slav republic, federated only in administration but centralized politically.

My attempt was not successful. I met the Polish democrats several times, but we could not agree, primarily because of a difference in our national concepts and feelings. They seemed to me narrow, limited, exclusive. They saw nothing but Poland, not understanding the changes that had taken place in Poland itself since its complete subjugation. In part we could not reach agreement because they did not trust me and they probably could promise themselves no great benefit from my assistance.[38] So, after several fruitless meetings in Versailles, we stopped seeing each other altogether, and my impulse, criminal in intent, this time could have no criminal consequence.

From the end of the summer of 1846 to November 1847 I again was completely inactive, busying myself with my studies as of old, following the growing movement in Europe with anxious attention, and burning with impatience to participate actively in it, but as yet undertaking nothing positive. I did not meet with the Polish democrats any more, but I did see many young Poles who had fled from their country in 1846 and almost all of whom subsequently turned to the mysticism of Mickiewicz. During the month of November I was ill and was staying at home with my head shaven when two of these young people came to me proposing that I deliver a speech at the ceremony held every year by Poles and Frenchmen in memory of the revolution of 1831. I grasped at this thought joyfully, ordered a wig, and having prepared a speech in three days delivered it before a large gathering on 17/29 November 1847. Sire! You perhaps are acquainted with this unfortunate speech, the beginning of my unfortunate and criminal adventures.* Because of it, at the demand of the Russian embassy, I was expelled from Paris and took up my residence in Brussels.[39]

* Nicholas' marginal note: "NB."

There Lelewel greeted me with a new fete; I delivered a second speech, which would have been published had not the February revolution intervened.[40] In this speech, which was, as it were, a development and continuation of the first, I spoke much of Russia, of her past development, much of the ancient enmity and struggle between Russia and Poland. I also spoke of the great future of the Slavs, who were summoned to renew the decaying Western world. Then, having reviewed the current situation in Europe and forecasting an imminent European revolution, a terrible storm, and especially the unavoidable destruction of the Austrian Empire, I ended with the following words: "Préparons-nous et quand l'heure aura sonné que chacun de nous fasse son devoir." *

Even then, however, except for mutual compliments and more or less agreeable phrases, and despite my strong desire to draw close to the Poles, I was unable to draw close to even one of them. Our natures, concepts, and sympathies were in too sharp contradiction for any real rapprochement between us to be possible. Moreover, at that very time the Poles had begun more than ever to view me with distrust: to my amazement and no small sorrow, for the first time the rumor spread that I was supposedly a secret agent of the Russian government. I later heard from the Poles that the Russian embassy in Paris, in response to a query about me from Minister Guizot,[41] was supposed to have replied, "C'est un homme qui ne manque pas de talent; nous l'employons, mais aujourd'hui il est allé trop loin," † and that Duchâtel ‡ let Prince Czartoryski know of this. I also heard that Minister Duchâtel had reported to the Belgian government that I was not a political émigré but simply a thief who, stealing a considerable sum in Russia and then fleeing, had been condemned to penal servitude for theft and flight. Be that as it may, these rumors, together with the other reasons mentioned above, made any relation between the Poles and me impossible.[42]

* "Let us prepare ourselves, and when the hour strikes let each of us do his duty."

† "He is a man who does not lack talent; we use him, but today he has gone too far."

‡ Polonskii has "Guizot."

In Brussels I was nearly drawn into the Society of United German and Belgian Communists and Radicals, with whom both the English Chartists and the French democrats were connected.[43] This society was not secret, however, but had public meetings; there were probably also secret gathe igs, but I did not participate in them, and I visited the public ones only twice all told. I then stopped going because I did not like the way they acted or their tone. And their demands were so intolerable to me that I even drew their displeasure upon myself, and, one might say, the hatred of the German communists, who began to shout more loudly than the others about my imaginary treachery. But I lived more in an aristocratic circle; I became acquainted with General Skrzynecki, and through him with Count Mérode, the former minister, and with the Frenchman Count Montalembert, the latter's son-in-law; that is, I lived in the very center of Jesuit propaganda.[44] They tried to convert me to the Catholic faith, and since, together with the Jesuits, there were some ladies who were also solicitious of my spiritual salvation, it was very pleasant for me in their company. At that time I was writing articles on Belgium and on the Belgian Jesuits for the *Constitutionnel*, not, however, ceasing to follow the accelerating course of political events in Italy and France.

At last the February revolution burst forth. No sooner had I learned that they were fighting in Paris than, taking an acquaintance's passport against any contingency, I set out again for France. But the passport was not necessary; the first word that greeted us at the border was: "La République est proclamée à Paris." * Chills ran up my spine when I heard this news. I arrived in Valenciennes on foot because the railroad had been cut. Everywhere there were crowds, wild shouts, red banners in all the streets and squares and on all public buildings. I had to go a roundabout way; the railroad was cut in many places. I arrived in Paris on 26 February, the third day after the proclamation of the republic. I enjoyed the trip. Now what shall I say to you, Sire, of the impression produced on

* "The Republic is proclaimed in Paris."

me by Paris! This huge city, the center of European enlightenment, had suddenly been turned into the wild Caucasus: on
every street, almost everywhere, barricades had been piled up
like mountains, reaching the roofs, and on them, among rocks
and broken furniture, like Lezghians * in ravines, workers in
their colorful blouses, blackened from powder and armed from
head to foot.† Fat shopkeepers, *épiciers* ‡ with faces stupid
from terror, timidly looked out of the windows. On the streets
and boulevards not a single carriage. And the dandies, young
and old, all the hated social lions with their walking sticks and
lorgnettes, had disappeared and in their place MY NOBLE
OUVRIERS in rejoicing, exulting crowds, with red banners and
patriotic songs, reveling in their victory! And in the midst of
this unlimited freedom, this mad rapture, all were so forgiv-
ing, sympathetic, loving of their fellow man—upright, modest, courteous, amiable, witty—that only in France, and in
France only in Paris, could one see such a thing! Later I lived
for more than a week with some workers in the Caserne de
Tournon, two steps from the Luxembourg Palace. These barracks were formerly the barracks of the Municipal Guard; at
this time they with many others were turned into a red republican fortress, into barracks for Caussidière's guard.[45] Now I
lived in them at the invitation of an acquaintance, a democrat
who commanded a detachment of five hundred workers. Thus
I had an opportunity to see and study these last from morning
till night. Sire! I assure you, in no class, never, and nowhere
have I found so much noble selflessness, so much truly touching integrity, such sincerely considerate good manners, and so
much amiable gaiety combined with such heroism as I found
in these simple, uneducated people, who always were and
always will be a thousand times better than all their leaders!
What is so striking about them is their deep instinct for discipline; in their barracks no established regimen, no laws, no
compulsion could exist, but God grant that any disciplined

* A tribe of the Caucasus Mountains.
† Nicholas' marginal note: "NB."
‡ Grocers.

soldier could so precisely obey, anticipate the wishes of his officers, and observe order as religiously as these free men. They demanded orders, they demanded leadership, they obeyed with punctiliousness, with fevor; they would perform heavy work for twenty-four hours at a stretch without eating and never grow despondent, but were always cheerful and amiable. If these people, if the French workers in general, found a leader worthy of them, one who was able to understand and love them, he could work wonders with them.

Sire! I am in no condition to give you a clear account of the month I spent in Paris, for it was a month of spiritual intoxication. Not only I but everyone was intoxicated: some from reckless fear, others from reckless rapture, from reckless hopes. I got up at five or even four in the morning and went to bed at two. I was on my feet all day, participated vigorously in all the meetings, gatherings, clubs, processions, outings, demonstrations; in a word, I imbibed with all my senses, through all my pores, the ecstatic atmosphere of revolution. It was a feast without beginning and without end. Here I saw everyone and saw no one because all were lost in one infinite, aimless crowd. I spoke with everyone, but I do not remember either what I said to them or what they said to me because at every step there were new topics, new adventures, new information. News that was arriving continually from the rest of Europe also helped no little to maintain and strengthen the general delirium. One constantly heard such things as, "On se bat à Berlin; le roi a pris la fuite, après avoir prononcé un discours! On s'est battu à Vienne, Metternich s'est enfui, la République y est proclamée! Toute l'Allemagne se soulève. Les italiens ont triomphé à Milan, à Venise; les autrichiens ont subi une honteuse défaite! La République y est proclamée; toute l'Europe devient République. Vive la République!" * It seemed that the whole world had been turned upside down.

* "They are fighting in Berlin; the King has taken flight after having made a speech! They have fought in Vienna, Metternich has fled, the Republic has been proclaimed there! All Germany is rising. The Italians have triumphed in Milan, in Venice; the Austrians have suffered a shameful defeat! The Republic has been proclaimed there; all Europe is becoming a republic. Long live the Republic!"

The inconceivable had become the usual, the impossible possible, and the possible and the usual unthinkable. In a word, minds were in such a state that if someone had arrived and said, "le bon Dieu vient d'être chassé du ciel, la République y est proclamée!" * then everyone would have believed him and no one would have been amazed. And it was not only the democrats who were in such a state of intoxication; on the contrary, the democrats were the first to become sober, for they had to get down to work and secure the power that had fallen into their hands by some unexpected miracle. The conservative party and the dynastic opposition, which in one day had become more conservative than the conservatives themselves—in a word, people of the old order believed in all miracles and all impossibilities more than did the democrats. They really thought that two times two had ceased to be four, and Thiers himself announced that "il ne nous reste plus qu'une chose, c'est de nous faire oublier." † This alone explains the haste and unanimity with which all cities, provinces, and classes in France accepted the republic.[46]

But it is time for me to return to my own story.

After two or three weeks of such intoxication I sobered up somewhat and began to ask myself: What shall I do now? My calling is not in Paris or in France, my place is on the Russian border; the Polish emigration is rushing there, preparing for war against Russia; I, too, must be there in order to influence both Russians and Poles at the same time, in order to keep the imminent war from turning into a war of Europe against Russia "pour refouler ce peuple barbare dans les déserts de l'Asie," ‡ as they put it on occasion; and to try to keep this from being not a war of Germanized Poles against the Russian people, but a Slav war, a war of free, united Slavs against the Russian Emperor.[47]

Sire! I shall not say a single word about the criminality and quixotic folly of my undertaking; I stop here only to define

* "The good Lord has just been chased out of heaven, the Republic has been proclaimed there!"
† "Only one thing remains for us: to make ourselves forgotten."
‡ To hurl back this barbarous people into the deserts of Asia.

more clearly my position, means, and connections at that time. I consider it necessary to enter into a detailed explanation on this score because I know that my departure from Paris was the object of many false accusations and suspicions.

First, I know that many have called me the agent of Ledru-Rollin.[48] Sire! In this testament I have concealed nothing from you, not a single sin, not a single crime. I have bared my whole soul to you. You have seen my errors, you have seen how I fell from folly into folly, from fault into sin, and from sin into crime. But you will believe me, Sire, when I tell you that with all my folly, with all the criminality of my designs and undertakings, I nonetheless retained too much pride, independence, feeling of my own worth, and finally too much love of my motherland to agree to act as a contemptible agent against her, as a blind and foul tool of any party whatsoever, of any person whatsoever! I have repeatedly explained in my depositions that I was scarcely acquainted with Ledru-Rollin, that I saw him only once in my life, and that I spoke hardly ten words with him—and they insignificant. And now I repeat the same thing because it is the truth. I was much more closely acquainted with Louis Blanc and Flocon, and I became acquainted with Albert [49] only after my return from France.* During the course of the entire month that I spent in Paris, I dined at Louis Blanc's three times and was in Flocon's house once, and also dined several times at the home of Caussidière, the revolutionary prefect of police, where I saw Albert several times. I did not see the other members of the Provisional Government at this time. There is only one circumstance that might give cause to the aforementioned accusation, but this circumstance apparently remained unknown to my accusers.

Having decided to travel to the Russian border and not having money for the trip, I long sought for some from friends and acquaintances; finding none, I reluctantly decided to have recourse to the democratic members of the Provisional Government. Consequently, I wrote and sent four copies of a short note with the following contents to Flocon, Louis Blanc, Al-

---

* Bakunin errs; he obviously means after his return to France from Belgium.

bert, and Ledru-Rollin: "Driven from France by the fallen government, and returning after the February revolution and now intending to travel to the Russian border, to the Duchy of Poznań, in order to act together with the Polish patriots, I am in need of money and request the democratic members of the Provisional Government to give me 2,000 francs, *not as gratuitous aid, for which I have no desire or right, but in the form of a loan,** promising to return this sum just as soon as possible." Receiving this note, Flocon asked me to come to him, and told me that he and his friends in the Provisional Government were ready to lend me this insignificant sum and more if I needed it, but that first he had to talk it over with the Polish Centralizacja, for, having binding relations with it, he was tied to it in everything that even somewhat concerned Poland. I do not know the nature of these talks or what the Polish democrats said to Flocon about me; I only know that the next day he offered me a considerably larger sum, that I took 2,000 francs from him, and that in bidding me farewell he asked me to write to him from Germany and Poland for his journal *La Réforme.* I wrote to him twice: from Cologne at the very beginning, then from Köthen at the very end of the year 1848 when I sent my *Appeal to the Slavs.*[50] I received neither letters nor assignments from him and had no other direct or indirect relations with him. I did not return the money because in Germany I lived in constant poverty.†

Second, I was accused, or rather, suspected—there were no positive facts for an accusation—suspected, I say, when I set out from Paris, of being in secret communication with the Polish democrats, of acting in concert with them, on their instructions and according to a previously formulated plan. Such suspicion was very natural, but also had no basis whatsoever. Among émigrés one must distinguish between two things: the noisy crowd and the secret societies, which always consist of a few enterprising people who lead the crowd with an invisible hand and prepare undertakings in secret meetings. I knew at

---

* Bakunin's italics.
† According to Polonskii, Nicholas wrote "NB" and made a line in the margin here; neither appears in Steklov.

this time a crowd of Polish émigrés and they knew me, knew me even better than I could know each of them, because they were countless and I was the only Russian among them. I heard what they said: their gasconades, fantasies, hopes. In a word, I heard what anyone could hear if only he wished to, but I did not participate in their meetings and was not trusted with the secrets of the actual conspirators. At that time in Paris there existed only two serious Polish societies: Czartoryski's society and the society of democrats. I never had any connections with Czartoryski's party, and I saw him only once. In 1846 I was about to enter into relations with the democratic Centralizacja, but my attempt was not successful, and in Paris after the February revolution I did not meet even one of its members. So at this time I knew much less of the intentions of the Polish democrats than of the contemporary Belgian, Italian, and especially German undertakings. Among the Italians I knew Mamiani and General Pepe, who did not belong to any societies at all. Among the Belgians I knew several leaders and heard of their intentions but did not interfere in their affairs. I was more closely and better acquainted with German affairs, for I was on friendly terms with Herwegh, who took an active part in them. I saw the beginning of Herwegh's unfortunate campaign to Baden. I knew of his means, his assistants, his arms, the promises of the Provisional Government, and the number of workers who enlisted in his regiment, and also his relations with the Baden democrats. I knew much because I was a friend to Herwegh, but in no way did I tie myself or my intentions to his intentions.[51]

To fill out the picture of my situation at that time and in order not to leave a single shadow of a lie in it, I must finally say a few words about the Russians too. Of course, in calling them my acquaintances I cannot compromise them more than they compromised themselves in Paris. Ivan Golovin, Nikolai Sazonov, Alexander Herzen,[52] and perhaps Nikolai Ivanovich Turgenev too—these were the only Russians with whom one might think, with some justification, that I had political relations. But I did not like or respect Golovin and always kept a great distance between us. And after the February revolution I believe I did not meet him even once. Nikolai Sazonov is an intelligent, knowledgeable, and gifted man, but he is excessively proud and egotistical. At first he was my enemy because I could not be convinced of the independence of the Russian aristocracy, of which he then considered himself not the last representative. Subsequently he came to call me his friend. I did not trust his friendship, but I did see him quite often, finding pleasure in his intelligent and amiable conversation. After my return from Belgium I met him several times at Herwegh's; he was sullen toward me and, as I heard later, was the first to spread rumors of my supposed dependence on Ledru-Rollin. Much closer to my heart was Herzen. He is a kind, noble, lively, witty man, something of a talker and an epicure. I saw him in Paris in the summer of 1847. He was then not yet thinking of emigrating and laughed more than the others at the tenor of my politics. He was concerned with all sorts of problems and topics, especially literature. At the end of the summer of 1847 he left for Italy and he returned to Paris in the summer of 1848, two or three months after my departure, so that we missed each other, never saw each other again, and did not correspond. Once he did send me some money, through Reichel. Finally, concerning N. I. Turgenev I can only say that now more than ever he was keeping apart from the whole world and as a wealthy proprietor and *rentier* was after all not a little frightened by the revolution that was taking place. I saw him cursorily and, one might say, in passing.

In a word, Sire, I can with complete justification say that I lived, undertook projects, and acted outside of any society, independently of any external inducement or influence: my folly, sins, and crimes belonged and belong exclusively to me. I am guilty of much, much, but I never stooped to be another's agent, the slave of another's thoughts.

Finally, there is still another vile accusation against me.

I have been accused of supposedly wanting—in association with two Poles whose names I have now forgotten—of supposedly intending to make an attempt on the life of Your Imperial Majesty. I shall not enter into the details of such a slander; I answered it in detail in my foreign depositions and am ashamed to say much about the subject.[53] I shall say only one thing, Sire: I am a criminal before you and before the law, I know the enormity of my crimes, but I also know that my soul was never capable of either villainy or baseness. My political fanaticism, existing more in my imagination than in my heart, also had its strongly defined limits, and Brutus, Ravaillac, and Alibaud were never my heroes.[54] Moreover, Sire, there was never even a shadow of hatred in my soul for you personally. When I was a cadet in the Artillery School, I, like all my comrades, loved you passionately. It used to be that when you came to our camp, just the words "The Sovereign is coming" would throw everyone into inexpressible rapture and all would rush to meet you. In your presence we did not know fear; on the contrary, near you and under your protection we sought refuge from our superiors; they would not dare follow us to Alexandria. I remember—it was during the cholera epidemic—you were sad, Sire. We surrounded you in silence, looked at you with timid reverence, and each of us felt your great sorrow in his soul, although we could not know its cause—and how happy was he to whom you would say a word! Then, many years later, when I was abroad and had already become an arrant democrat, I began to feel obliged to hate Emperor Nikolai; but this hatred was in my imagination, in my thoughts, and not in my heart. I hated an abstract political person, the personification of autocratic power in Russia, the oppressor of Poland, and not that majestic living person who affected me deeply in the very beginning of my life and impressed himself upon my youthful heart. The impressions of youth are not easily effaced, Sire! And even at the very height of my political fanaticism my folly kept within certain bounds; my attacks upon you never went beyond the political sphere. I dared call you a cruel, iron, merciless despot. I preached hatred for and rebellion against your authority, but I never dared or wished and never could speak with sacrilegious tongue specifically of your person, Sire; and I do not find words to express this, but I deeply feel the distinction— never, in a word, did I speak or write like a base lackey who curses his lord and censures and slanders him because he knows that his master does not hear him or is too far away to strike him with his cudgel. Finally, Sire, even in the most recent times, in defiance of all democratic concepts and as though against my will, I deeply, deeply respected you! Not I alone, many others—Poles and Europeans in general—realized with me that among the presently reigning crowned heads, only you, Sire, have kept faith in your regal calling. With such feelings, with such thoughts, despite all my political folly, I could not be a regicide, and you will believe, Sire, that this accusation is nothing but vile slander.

And now I return to my narrative.

Having taken money from Flocon, I went to Caussidière for a passport. I obtained from him not one but two passports— just in case—one in my own name, the other under an alias, wishing to keep secret as far as possible my presence in Germany and in the Duchy of Poznań. Then, having dined at Herwegh's and having received letters and instructions from him to the Baden democrats, I took a seat in a diligence and set out for Strasbourg. If someone in the diligence had asked me about the purpose of my trip and I had wanted to reply, then the following conversation might have taken place between us.

"For what purpose are you traveling?"

"To rebel."

"Against whom?"

"Against Emperor Nikolai."

"How?"

"I don't really know yet."

"Just where are you going now?"

"To the Duchy of Poznań."

"Why specifically there?"

"Because I have heard from the Poles that there is more life there now, more movement, and it is easier to have an effect on the Kingdom of Poland from there than from Galicia."

"What are your means?"

"Two thousand francs."

"And your hopes for means?"

"No definite ones, but perhaps I'll find some."

"Do you have acquaintances and connections in the Duchy of Poznań?"

"Except for a few young people whom I met rather often at the University of Berlin, I don't know anyone there."

"Do you have letters of recommendation?"

"Not a one."

"Just how do you—without means and alone—plan to fight the Russian Tsar?"

"The revolution is with me, and in Posen I hope to escape from my solitude."

"All the Germans are now shouting against Russia, elevating the Poles, and with them are preparing to war against the Russian Tsardom. You are a Russian. Can it be that you will unite with them?"

"God preserve me! If the Germans even dare set foot on Slav soil, I shall become their implacable enemy. But it is just for this that I am going to Posen: to oppose with all my power the unnatural alliance of Poles and Germans against Russia."

"But the Poles alone are in no position to fight Russian power, are they?"

"Alone, no, but in union with other Slavs, especially if I succeed in carrying with me the Russians in the Kingdom of Poland . . ."

"On what are your hopes based? Do you have connections with Russians?"

"None, but I rely on propaganda and on the mighty spirit of revolution that has now taken possession of the whole world!"

Not speaking of the magnitude of the crime, it must be very amusing to you, Sire, that I—alone, nameless, and powerless—was going to do battle against you, the Great Tsar of a Great Tsardom! Now I clearly see my folly, and I myself would laugh if I felt up to laughing; and I recall willy-nilly one of the fables of Ivan Andreevich Krylov. . . .[55] But then I saw nothing and did not want to think of anything, and moved as one possessed toward my obvious destruction. And if anything can even somewhat excuse the absurdity of my escapade—I do not say the criminality—then perhaps it is simply the fact that I came from intoxicated Paris, was intoxicated myself, yes, and that everybody around me was intoxicated!

Arriving in Frankfurt early in April, I found there a countless number of Germans who had come from all parts of Germany for the Vorparlament.[56] I made the acquaintance of almost all the democrats, handed over Herwegh's letters and
instructions, and set about observing, trying to find some
sense in the German chaos and at least a germ of unity in this
new building of the Tower of Babel. I spent about a week in
Frankfurt, was in Mainz, Mannheim, and Heidelberg. I wit-
nessed many popular armed and unarmed gatherings; I visited
German clubs. I knew personally the principal leaders of the
Baden uprising and knew of all the undertakings but did not
take an active part in a single one of them, although I sympa-
thized with them and wished them all success. In all that concerned me personally and my own plans, I remained as before
in complete isolation. Then, on the way to Berlin, I spent several days in Cologne, waiting for my things to arrive from
Brussels. The farther north I got, the colder I became spiri-
tually.[57] In Cologne I was seized by an inexpressible depression, a premonition, as it were, of my coming destruction! But
nothing could stop me. The day after my arrival in Berlin I was
arrested, at first being taken for Herwegh * and then as punishment for traveling with two passports. I was detained for
only one day, however, and then released, having given my
word that I would not go to the Duchy of Poznań and that I
would not stay in Berlin but would go to Breslau. Chief of
Police Minutoli kept the passport made out in my own name
but returned to me the other in the name of the nonexistent
Leonhard Neglinski. Personally he gave me yet another passport in the name of Wolf or Hoffman, I don't remember which,
probably not wanting me to get out of the habit of traveling
with two passports. So, having seen almost nothing in Berlin
except the police station, I set out again and arrived in Breslau
at the end of April or the very beginning of May.[58]

I remained in Breslau uninterruptedly right up to the Slav
Congress; i.e., until the end of May, almost a month. My first

---

* Steklov notes that an asterisk is drawn in pencil under the name Herwegh.

task was to make the acquaintance of the Breslau democrats; the second was to search out Poles with whom I could unite. The first was easy, but the second not only was difficult but proved to be positively impossible. At this time many Poles were assembling in Breslau from Galicia, from Kraków, from the Duchy of Poznań, and finally émigrés from Paris and London. It was something of a Polish congress.[59] This congress had no important results, at least as far as I know. I did not attend its sessions, but I heard that there was much noise, violent discord, and differences among the provinces and parties, as a result of which all the Poles dispersed, having made no substantial decisions. My position among them was difficult and strange from the very beginning: all knew me, were very amiable, and paid me a host of compliments, but I felt alien among them. The sweeter their words, the colder I felt in my heart, and neither I and they nor they and I could get together. Moreover, at this very time—for the second time and more strongly than the first—the rumor of my supposed treachery spread among them. The émigrés more than anyone else—especially the members of the democratic society—believed this rumor and spread it. Subsequently, much later, they apologized, placing all guilt on that old gossip Count Ledóchowski, who had supposedly been warned by Lamartine and who had rushed to warn all the Polish democrats.[60] The Poles grew visibly cold toward me, and I, finally losing patience, began to draw away from them, so that until the Prague Congress I did not have any relations with them, saw only a few of them, without any political aim.

To make up for this, I was with the Germans more often; I visited their democratic club, and at this time enjoyed such popularity among them that solely through my efforts Arnold Ruge, my old friend, was chosen by Breslau [as a delegate] to the Frankfurt National Assembly. The Germans are a comical but good people and I have almost always been able to get along with them, excluding, however, the littérateurs-communists. At this time the Germans were playing at politics and they listened to me as to an oracle. There were no conspiracies or serious undertakings among them, but much noise, singing, beer drinking, and boastful chatter. Everything was done and said openly on the street. There were no laws, no leadership: complete freedom, and every evening, as though for entertainment, a little uprising. Their clubs were nothing but exercises in eloquence or, to put it better, empty talk.

During all of May I remained completely idle; I was bored and melancholy and was awaiting the opportune moment. The political conditions at this time contributed no little to my despondency: the unsuccessful uprising of the Duchy of Poznań, although it was shameful for the Prussian troops, the expulsion of the Poles (émigrés) from Kraków and soon thereafter from Prussia as well, the complete shipwreck of the Baden democrats, and finally the first defeat of the democrats in Paris were obvious portents of the ebb of revolution that had already then begun. The Germans did not see this and did not understand, but I understood and for the first time doubted success. Finally they began to talk about the Slav Congress; I decided to go to Prague, hoping to find there an Archimedean fulcrum for action.[61]

Up to this time, excluding the Poles and not speaking of the Russians, I was not acquainted with a single Slav, and also I had never been in the Austrian domains. I knew about the Slavs from the accounts of several eyewitnesses and from books. I also had heard in Paris of a club found by Cyprien Robert,[62] who had replaced Mickiewicz in the chair of Slavic Literatures, but I did not go to this club, not wishing to mix with Slavs who were led by a Frenchman. Acquaintance and close friendship with Slavs was therefore a new experience for me, and I expected much from the Prague congress, hoping especially to overcome, with the aid of the other Slavs, the narrowness of Polish national pride.

Although my expectations were not fully realized, they were not entirely disappointed. Slavs, in the political sense, are children, but I found an incredible freshness and incomparably more natural intelligence and energy in them than in the Germans. It was touching to see them meet, their childish yet profound delight; one would say that the members of one and the same family, scattered by a terrible fate throughout the whole world, were meeting for the first time after a long and bitter separation. They wept, they laughed, they embraced— and in their tears, in their joy, in their cordial greetings there was no phrasemaking, no falseness, no high-flown bombast. Everything was simple, sincere, sacred. In Paris I had been carried away by democratic exaltation and by the heroism of the common people; here I was carried away by the sincerity and warmth of simple yet profound Slavic feeling. The Slav heart in me awoke, and for the first time I was ready to forget almost completely all democratic sympathies tying me to Western Europe. The Poles viewed the other Slavs from the height of their own political importance and held themselves somewhat apart, smiling slightly. I, however, mixed with them and lived with them and shared their joy with all my soul, with all my heart. And therefore I was liked by them and enjoyed their almost universal confidence.

The predominant feeling among the Slavs is hatred for the Germans. The energetic albeit discourteous expression "damned German," pronounced in all Slav languages in almost the same manner, produces an incredible effect on every Slav. I tested its power several times and saw it vanquish even the Poles. Sometimes it was enough to curse the Germans at an opportune moment for them to forget both their Polish exclusiveness and their hatred for the Russians, as well as the cunning though useless policy * that compelled them to flirt often with the Germans. In a word, it was sometimes enough to tear them completely from that cramped, morbid, artificially cold shell in which they live against their will, as a result of their great national misfortunes; to awaken in them a lively Slav heart and cause them to feel as one with all Slavs. In Prague, where there was no end to the defamation of the Germans, I felt myself closer even to the Poles. Hatred for the Germans was the inexhaustible topic of all conversation; it served instead of a greeting among strangers. When two Slavs met,

---

* Steklov notes that the copyist erred here; Polonskii perpetrates the copyist's error in writing "though not useless policy."

the first word between them was almost always against the Germans, as though to assure one another that they were both true, good Slavs. Hatred for the Germans is the primary basis of Slav unity and mutual understanding among the Slavs. It is so strong, so deeply engraved in the heart of every Slav, that I am even now convinced, Sire, that sooner or later, in some way or another, no matter how political relationships in Europe are defined, the Slavs will throw off the German yoke, and the time will come when there will be no Prussian or Austrian or Turkish Slavs.

In my opinion, the importance of the Slav Congress lay in the fact that this was the first meeting, the first acquaintance, the first effort at union and understanding of the Slavs among themselves. As far as the congress itself is concerned, it—just like all other contemporary congresses and political gatherings—was decidedly empty and meaningless. Of the origin of the Slav Congress I know the following.

Since ancient times there had existed in Prague a learned literary circle that had as its goal the preservation, elevation, and development of Czech literature, Czech national customs, and also the distinctive essence of the Slav nations in general, which is repressed, restricted, and disdained by the Germans as well as by the Magyars. This circle was in lively and continual communication with similar circles among the Slovaks, Croatians, Slovenes, Serbs, and even the Lusatians in Saxony and Prussia, and was, so to speak, their head. Palacký, Šafařík, Count Thun, Hanka, Kollár, Hurban, L'udovit Štúr, and several others were the leaders of Slav propaganda, at first literary but then attaining political significance.[63] The Austrian government did not like them, but tolerated them because they counteracted the Magyars. As evidence and as an example of their activity I shall cite only one circumstance: Ten—no more than fifteen—years ago in Prague, no one, absolutely not a soul, spoke Czech, with the possible exception of the rabble and the workmen. Everyone spoke German and lived like Germans; they were ashamed of the Czech language and of their Czech origins. Now, on the contrary, not a single man, woman, or child wants to speak German, and in Prague the Germans themselves have learned to understand and express themselves in Czech. I have given only Prague as an example, but the same thing has taken place in all the other Bohemian, Moravian, and Slovak cities, large and small; the villages, of course, never ceased living and speaking like Slavs.

You, Sire, know how deep and powerful are the sympathies of the Slavs toward the mighty Russian Tsardom upon whose support and assistance they have relied, and to what extent the Austrian government and the Germans in general have feared and do fear Russian Pan-Slavism! In recent years the innocent literary-scholarly circle has expanded, become stronger, captured and carried along with itself all the youth, and has put down roots in the popular masses—and the literary movement has suddenly turned into a political one. The Slavs were only waiting for an opportunity to show themselves to the world.

In the year 1848 this opportunity was found. The Austrian Empire was about to disintegrate into its very diverse, antagonistic, incompatible elements, and if it was saved in time, then it was not by its own decrepit strength, only by your help, Sire! The Italians rebelled, the Magyars and the Germans rebelled, finally the Slavs rebelled too. The Austrian, or better, the Innsbruck government (for there were then many Austrian governments, at least two: the actual one in Innsbruck, the other official and constitutional one in Vienna, to say nothing of the third—the Hungarian—also officially called a government); and so the dynastic government in Innsbruck, abandoned by all and deprived of almost all its means, began to look for its salvation in the national movement of the Slavs.

The first thought of assembling a Slav Congress in Prague belongs to the Czechs, and specifically to Šafařík, Palacký, and Count Thun.[64] In Innsbruck they seized upon it with joy because they hoped that the Slav Congress would serve as an antidote to the congress of the Germans in Frankfurt. Count Thun, Palacký, and Brauner[65] then created in Prague something in the way of a provisional government; they were recognized by Innsbruck and treated with it directly, bypassing the Vienna ministers, whom they wanted neither to recognize nor to obey, seeing in them hostile representatives of German nationalism. Thus there was formed a semiofficial Czech party, half Slav and half governmental—governmental because it wanted to save the dynasty, the monarchic principle, and the integrity of the Austrian monarchy. It did not want to do this unconditionally, however, but demanded in return, first, a constitution; second, the transfer of the imperial capital from Vienna to Prague (which was actually promised them, of course with the firm intention of not keeping the promise); and finally the complete transformation of the Austrian monarchy from a German into a Slav monarchy, so that no longer should the Germans or the Magyars oppress the Slavs, but the reverse. In his brochure that appeared at that time, Palacký expressed all this in the following words: "Wir wollen das Kunststück versuchen, die bis zu ihrem tiefsten Wesen erschütterte Monarchie auf unserem slavischen Boden und mit unserer slavischen Kraft zu beleben, zu heilen und zu befestigen" *—an impossible undertaking in which they must have been either deceived or deceivers.

But the Czech party was not satisfied with this general predominance of the Slav element in the Austrian Empire. Relying on its semiofficial character and on the ingratiating Innsbruck promises, it also wanted to organize in its interest something on the order of Czech hegemony and affirm among the Slavs themselves the predominance of the Czech language and of the principal features of Czech national life. To say nothing of Moravia, it intended to annex to Bohemia the Slovak land, Austrian Silesia, and even Galicia, threatening the Poles, in case they did not submit, with inciting the Ruthenes to rebel; in a word, they wanted to create a powerful Bohemian kingdom.[66]

Such were the pretensions of the Czech politicians. They of course met strong opposition among the Slovaks, the Silesians,

* "We want to attempt the clever trick of animating, healing, and strengthening on our Slav ground and with our Slav strength the [Austrian] monarchy, which is convulsed to its depths." (Polonskii has "Osterreichische Monarchie"; not in Steklov.) This passage is not found in any of Palacký's published works or addresses of 1848–1849. The general tenor, however, corresponds to Palacký's concept of Austro-Slavism.

and most of all the Poles. The last came to Prague not at all to submit to the Czechs or, if the truth be told, because of any extraordinary attraction to their Slav brothers or to Slav thought, but simply in the hope of finding support and assistance for their own particular national undertakings. Thus from the very first days a struggle took place, not among the masses of Slavs who had come, but only among their leaders, and most of all a struggle between the Poles and the Czechs, between the Poles and the Ruthenes—a struggle that came to naught, just as did the whole Slav Congress. The South Slavs were averse to all debates and were occupied exclusively with preparations for the Hungarian war, trying to persuade the other Slavs to set aside all internal questions until the complete deposition of the Magyars or, as others said, until the complete expulsion of the latter from Hungary. The Poles did not agree to either one or the other, but proposed their own mediation, which neither the South Slavs nor, so far as I heard, the Magyars themselves wanted to accept. In a word, everyone was pulling in his own direction and wished to make of the others a steppingstone for his own advancement: the Czechs most of all—spoiled by the flattery of Innsbruck—and then the Poles, too, spoiled not by fate but by the flattery of the European democrats.

The congress consisted of three sections: the *Northern*, in which were the Poles, Ruthenes, Silesians; the *Western*, consisting of the Czechs, Moravians, Slovaks; and the *Southern*, in which the Serbs, Croats, Slovenes, and Dalmatians met.[67] According to the original formulation of Palacký, the main creator and director of the Slav Congress, this congress was to consist exclusively of Austrian Slavs, and the non-Austrians were to attend only as guests. But this formulation was rejected at the very start; there entered the congress, not as guests but as active members, many Poles from Poznań, Polish émigrés, several Turkish Serbs, and finally two Russians: I and one Old Ritualist priest whose name I have forgotten; it can, however, be found in Šafařík's printed account of the Slav Congress.[68] The priest, or rather monk, was from an old Ritualist monastery in Bukovina, with its own special metropolitan, and was apparently eliminated at this very time upon demand of the Russian government. He had traveled with the dismissed metropolitan to Vienna, and then, hearing of the Slav Congress, came alone to Prague.

I entered the Northern—that is, the Polish—section, and on entering delivered a brief speech in which I said that Russia, in tearing itself away from its Slav brothers by enslaving Poland and especially in betraying her into the hands of the Germans, the common and chief enemies of the whole Slav race, cannot return to Slav unity and brotherhood except by liberating Poland, and that for this reason my place in the Slav Congress had to be among the Poles.[69] The Poles received me with applause and chose me as deputy to the South Slav section, in accordance with my own wish. The Old Ritualist priest entered the section of the Poles with me, and on my intercession was even elected by them to the Plenary Committee, which consisted of deputies from the three main groups. I shall not hide from you, Sire, that the thought of using this priest for revolutionary propaganda in Russia entered my mind. I knew that there were many Old Ritualists and other schismatics in Rus' and that the Russian people are inclined toward religious fanaticism. Now my priest was a sly and clever man, a real Russian knave and a rascal. He had spent some time in Moscow, knew much about the Old Ritualists and much in general about the schismatics in the Russian Empire, and it seems that his monastery was in continuous communication with the Russian Old Ritualists. But I did not have time to concern myself with him; I rather doubted the morality of such an association. I still did not have a definite plan of action, I did not yet have contacts, and, most important, I did not have money. And without money there is no point in talking with such people. Moreover, at this time I was exclusively occupied with the Slav question. I saw him seldom, and later completely lost sight of him.

Days flowed by and the congress did not move. The Poles were busy with regulations, parliamentary procedures, and the Ruthenian question. The more important questions were discussed not at the congress but at special meetings, which were not so numerous. I did not participate in these meetings;

I heard only that at them the Breslau dissensions were continued in part and that there was much talk of Kossuth and of the Magyars, with whom, if I am not mistaken, the Poles were already beginning to have positive relations at this time, to the great displeasure of the other Slavs.[70] The Czechs were occupied with their own ambitious plans, the South Slavs with the impending war. Few thought of the common Slav problem. I became depressed again and I began to feel as isolated in Prague as I had earlier in Paris and Germany. I spoke several times in the Polish and South Slav sections and also in the Plenary Committee. Here is the main content of my speeches:

"Why have you come together in Prague? Is it to talk here of your provincial interests? Or is it to merge all special causes of the Slav peoples, their interests, demands, and problems, into one indivisible, great Slav question? Begin to concern yourselves with it, and subordinate all your special demands to the Slav cause. Our assembly is the first Slav assembly. We must lay here the beginning of a new Slav life, proclaim and affirm the unity of all Slav nations, united henceforth in one indivisible and great political body.

"And first let us ask ourselves if our assembly is only an assembly of Austrian Slavs, or is it a Slav assembly in general? What is the sense of the expression 'Austrian Slavs'? Slavs living in the Austrian Empire, no more—or, if you like, then perhaps Slavs enslaved by the Austrian Germans. Now if you wish to limit your assembly to representatives of the Austrian Slavs only, then by what right do you call it a Slav assembly? You exclude all the Slavs of the Russian Empire, the Slavs subject to Prussia, the Turkish Slavs; the minority excludes the huge majority, yet dares call itself Slav! Call yourselves German Slavs and your congress a congress of German slaves, but not a Slav congress.

"I know that many of you hope for the support of the Austrian dynasty. It promises you everything now, it flatters you because you are necessary to it; but will it keep its promises and will it be possible for it to keep them when, with your help, it restores its fallen power? You say that it will keep them, but I am convinced that it will not.

"The first law of any government is the law of self-preservation; all moral laws are subordinate to it, and there has not yet been an example in history of a government keeping promises it made in a critical moment unless it was forced to do so. You will see that the Austrian dynasty not only will forget your services but will avenge itself upon you for its past shameful weakness, which forced it to humble itself before you and flatter your seditious demands. The history of the Austrian dynasty is richer than others in such examples, and you learned Czechs, you who know so well and in such detail the past misfortunes of your motherland, you should understand better than others that it is not love for the Slavs, or love for Slav independence, or for the Slavic language, or for Slav mores and customs, but only iron necessity that makes it seek your friendship now.

"Finally, assuming even the impossible, assuming that the Austrian dynasty really wants and is in a position to keep the word it has given, what will your gains be? Austria will be transformed from a half-German into a half-Slav state; that means that you will be turned from the oppressed into the oppressors, from haters into hated. It means that you not numerous Austrian Slavs will break away from the Slav majority, that you yourselves will destroy any hope for Slav unification, that great Slav unity which, at least in your words, is the first and main object of your desires. Slav unity, Slav freedom, Slav rebirth are possible in no other way than through the complete destruction of the Austrian Empire.

"No less mistaken are those who, for the restoration of Slav independence, hope for the assistance of the Russian Tsar. The Russian Tsar has concluded a new close alliance with the Austrian dynasty, not for you but against you, not to help you but to return you forcibly—you as well as all other rebelling Austrian subjects—to your old subject status, to your old absolute obedience. Emperor Nikolai does not like either freedom of the peoples or constitutions; you have seen a living example of this in Poland. I know that the Russian government has long cultivated you, as well as the Turkish Slavs, through its agents who travel about the Slav lands, spreading Pan-Slav ideas among you, seducing you with the hope of imminent assistance, of the supposedly approaching liberation of all Slavs through the mighty power of the Russian Tsardom. And I do not doubt that it sees in the distant, the very distant future, a moment when all the Slav lands will become part of the Russian Empire. But none of us will live until the long-wished-for hour. Do you want to wait until then? Not you alone, but the Slav nations will have time to become decrepit before that time. But now there is no place for you in the womb of the Russian Tsardom. You want life, but deathly silence is there; you demand independence, movement, but mechanical obedience is there. You desire resurrection, elevation, enlightenment, but death, darkness, and slavish labor are there. Entering the Russia of Emperor Nikolai you would enter the tomb of all national life and of all freedom. It is true that without Russia Slav unity is not complete and there is no Slav power; but it would be senseless to expect salvation and assistance for the Slavs from present-day Russia. What is left for you? First, unite outside of Russia, not excluding her but waiting, hoping for her speedy liberation; and she will be carried away by your example and you will be the liberators of the Russian people, who in turn will then be your strength and your shield.

"Begin your unification in the following manner: proclaim that you Slavs—not Austrian but living on Slav land in the so-called Austrian Empire—have gathered and united in Prague to lay the first foundation for the future free and great federation of all Slav peoples; and that in expectation that your Slav brothers in the Russian Empire, in the Prussian possessions, and in Turkey will join you, you Czechs, Moravians, Poles from Galicia and Kraków, Ruthenes, Silesians, Slovaks, Serbs, Slovenes, Croats, and Dalmatians have concluded among yourselves a strong and indissoluble, defensive and offensive union on the following bases." [71]

I shall not enumerate here all the points I thought of; I shall say only that this project, subsequently printed—without my knowledge, however, and only in part—in one of the Czech journals, was drawn up in a democratic spirit; that it left much scope for national and provincial differences in all that concerned administration, assuming even here, however, certain basic formulations common and binding for all; but that in everything concerning internal as well as external policy, power was to be transferred to and concentrated in the hands of a central government.[72] Thus both the Poles and the Czechs would have to disappear, with all their selfish and vain pretensions, in the general Slav union. I also advised the congress to demand from the Innsbruck court, which was still conceding everything, official recognition of the union as well as the same concessions that it had not long before made to the Magyars and hence could not deny to its good and faithful Slavs, namely, a special Slav ministry, special Slav troops with Slav officers, and special Slav finances. I also advised demanding the return of Croatian and other Slav regiments from Italy; finally, I advised sending a representative to Hungary, to Kossuth, not in the name of Ban Jelačić,[73] but in the name of all united Slavs, in order to solve the Magyar-Slav question in a peaceful manner and propose to the Magyars as well as to the Transylvanian Vlachs [74] that they enter a Slav or, if you will, an eastern republican union, with rights equal to those of all Slavs.

I confess, Sire, that in offering such a project to the Slav Congress I had in view the complete destruction of the Austrian Empire, its destruction in either case: in case of forced agreements and also in case of refusal, which would bring the dynasty into fatal collision with the Slavs. My other main goal was to find in the united Slavs a point of departure for broad revolutionary propaganda in Russia for the beginning of the struggle against you, Sire! I could not join with the Germans; that would have meant a European war and, even worse, a war of Germany against Russia. Neither could I join with the Poles: they had little faith in me; and as for me, when I became more closely acquainted with their national character, their incurable egotism, although it is historically understandable to me, I myself became ashamed and utterly incapable of mixing with the Poles, of acting with them as one against my motherland. On the contrary, in a Slav union I saw a fatherland, but a broader one in which, if only Russia were to join it, both the Poles and the Czechs would have to yield first place to her.

I have used the expression "revolutionary propaganda in Russia" several times; and at last it is time for me to explain how I understood this propaganda and what hopes and means I had for it. First of all, Sire, I must solemnly proclaim to you that not earlier, or at this time, or later was there any communication or even the shadow or even the beginning of relations with Russia or with Russians or with a single person living within the borders of your Empire. Since 1842 I had not received more than ten letters from Russia and I scarcely wrote that many, and in these letters there was not even a trace of politics. In 1848 I was on the point of hoping to enter into relations with Russians living on the borders of Poznań and Galicia. For this I needed the assistance of the Poles, but, as I have already explained several times, I could not or did not know how to get along with the Poles. I was not once in the Duchy of Poznań or in Kraków or in Galicia, nor did I know a single inhabitant of these provinces of whom I could positively and in good conscience say that he had relations with the Kingdom of Poland or with the Ukraine. Moreover, I do not think that the Poles at this time had frequent relations with the border provinces of the Russian Empire: they complained of the difficulty of communication, of the living, impassable wall with which it had surrounded itself. There were only obscure, for the most part senseless, rumors. Thus, for instance, at one time a rumor spread of an uprising in Moscow and of a supposed newly discovered Russian plot; another time that Russian officers had allegedly smashed the cannon in the Warsaw citadel, and similar nonsense that I, despite all the folly into which I myself had sunk, never believed.

All my undertakings remained in my thoughts, not because I did not wish to act, but because I was unable to, having neither ways nor means for propaganda. Count Orlov has told me that the government was informed that I supposedly spoke when abroad of my connections with Russia, especially with Little Russia. To this I can say only one thing: I never liked to

lie and therefore I did not speak and could not speak of connections that I did not have. I heard of the Ukraine from Polish
landowners living in Galicia. I heard that, supposedly as a
consequence of the liberation of the Galician peasants at the
beginning of 1848, the Little Russian peasants in Volynia, in
Podolia, as well as in Kiev province, were so strongly agitated
that many landowners, fearing for their lives, left for Odessa.[75]
This is positively all that I heard about Little Russia. It is quite
possible that I later spoke publicly of this news because I
grasped resolutely at anything that could even slightly support
or, better, awaken in the European and especially in the Slav
public a belief in the possibility, the necessity of a Russian
revolution.

I must make one observation here.

Doomed by my previous life—by my ideas, my position, my
unsatisfied need for action, and also by my will—to an unhappy revolutionary career, I could not tear away my nature or
my heart or my thoughts from Russia. As a consequence of
this I could not have another sphere of action besides Russia;
as a consequence of this I had to believe—or, better, I had to
make myself and others believe—in a Russian revolution.
What I said in this letter concerning Mickiewicz can perhaps
also be applied to me, although not to the same extent: I was
at that time deceived and a deceiver, I deluded myself and
others, doing violence, as it were, to my own mind and to the
common sense of my listeners. By nature I am not a charlatan,
Sire; on the contrary, nothing is so repugnant to me as charlatanry, and thirst for the pure and simple truth never died in
me. But the unnatural, unhappy position to which I had nevertheless brought myself sometimes forced me to be a charlatan against my will. Without connections, without means,
alone with my schemes in the midst of a crowd of strangers, I
had only one companion in arms: my faith. And I said to
myself that faith moves mountains, destroys obstacles, vanquishes the invincible, and performs the impossible; that faith
alone is half of success, half of victory. Coupled with a strong
will, it gives rise to circumstances, it gives rise to people, it
gathers, unites, and merges the masses into one soul and one

power. I said to myself that believing in a Russian revolution and having caused others—Europeans, especially Slavs, and consequently Russians too—to believe in it, I would make a revolution in Russia possible and unavoidable. In a word, I wanted to believe and I wanted others to believe too. I acquired this false, artificial, forced faith not without toil and painful struggle. More than once, in lonely moments, torturous doubts—doubts as to the morality and the possibility of my undertaking—came upon me. More than once I heard an inner, reproachful voice, and more than once I repeated to myself the words spoken to the Apostle Paul when he was still called Saul: "It is hard for thee to kick against the pricks." * But all was in vain; I stifled my conscience and rejected my doubts as unworthy. I knew Russia but little; I had been living abroad for eight years, and when I did live in Russia I was so exclusively occupied with German philosophy that I saw nothing around me. Moreover, the study of Russia without special assistance from the government is difficult, almost impossible, even to those who try to know her. And the study of the simple people, the peasants, seems to me difficult even for the government.

When I was abroad and my attention turned to Russia for the first time, I began to recall and collect old, unconscious impressions. Partly from them and partly from various rumors that were reaching me, stretching or trimming every fact and every circumstance on the Procrustean bed of my democratic desires, I created for myself a Russia of fantasy, ready for revolution. In this way I deceived myself and others. Of my connections or of my influence in Russia, I never spoke: this would have been a lie and a lie was repugnant to me. But when those about me supposed that I had influence, that I had definite connections, I remained silent and did not contradict them, for in their opinions I found almost the only support for my undertakings. In this way there must have come about many idle, baseless rumors that probably later reached the government.

* Acts 9:5 and 26:14.

And so there was no Russian propaganda even in embryo; it existed only in my thoughts. But in what manner did it exist in my thoughts? I shall attempt to reply to this question with all possible sincerity and detail. Sire! These avowals will be difficult for me! It is not that I fear they will awaken the righteous anger of Your Imperial Majesty and bring upon me the cruelest punishment; since 1848, and especially since the time of my imprisonment, I have succeeded in passing through so many different conditions and impressions—expectations, bitter experiences and bitter forebodings, hopes, fears, and terrors—that finally my soul has burned out, become dull, and it seems to me that both hope and terror have lost all influence on it! No, Sire, but it is painful, shameful, and disgraceful for me to speak to you directly of the crimes I contemplated against you personally and against Russia, although these crimes were crimes only in thought and intention and never became acts.

If I stood before you, Sire, only as before a Tsar-judge, I could relieve myself of this internal torment without entering into useless details. For a just application of penal laws it would be enough if I said: "I wanted with all my strength and by all possible means to inspire a revolution in Russia; I wanted to burst into Russia and rebel against the sovereign and destroy the existing order completely. If I did not rebel and did not begin propaganda, then it was solely because I did not have the means for this, and not for lack of will." The law would be satisfied, for such an admission is sufficient to condemn me to the cruelest punishment existing in Russia. But because of your extraordinary mercy, Sire, I stand now not as before a Tsar-judge but as before a Tsar-confessor, and I must show him all the secret hiding places of my mind. I shall confess myself before you. I shall try to bring light into the chaos of my thoughts and feelings so as to set them forth in order; I shall speak before you as though I were speaking before God Himself, whom it is impossible to deceive by either flattery or lies. And I entreat you, Sire! Permit me to forget for a minute that I stand before the great and terrible Tsar before whom millions tremble and in whose presence no one dares not only to speak but even to have an opposing opinion! Let me think that I am now speaking only before my spiritual father.

I wanted a revolution in Russia. *First question:* Why did I wish this? *Second question:* What order of things did I wish in place of the existing order? And finally, the *third question:* With what means and in what ways did I think to begin a revolution in Russia?

When you travel about the world you find everywhere much evil, oppression, and injustice, and in Russia perhaps more than in other states. It is not that people in Russia are worse than in Western Europe; on the contrary, I think the Russian is better, kinder, and has greater breadth of soul than the westerner. But in the West there is a specific against evil: publicity, public opinion, and finally, freedom, which ennobles and elevates every man. This remedy does not exist in Russia. Western Europe sometimes seems worse because there every evil comes out into the open, little remains secret. But in Russia all illnesses turn inward and eat away the innermost structure of the social organism. In Russia the prime mover is fear; and fear kills all life, all intelligence, all noble movement of the soul. It is difficult and painful for a man who loves truth to live in Russia: for a man who loves his neighbor; for a man who respects the worth and independence of the immortal soul in all men equally; for a man who, in a word, suffers not only from persecution of which he himself is a victim but also from persecution that falls upon his neighbor! Russian social life is a chain of mutual oppressions: the higher oppresses the lower; the latter suffers, does not dare complain, but he in turn squeezes the one who is still lower, who also suffers and also takes revenge on the one subordinate to him. Worst of all is it for the common people, the poor Russian muzhik, who, at the very bottom of the social ladder, has no one to oppress and must suffer oppression from all; as the Russian proverb says, "Only the lazy man does not beat us." *

People steal and take bribes and perpetrate injustice for

* "Nas tol'ko lenivii ne b'et."

money everywhere! In France and England, and even in honest Germany, but in Russia, I believe, more than in other states. In the West the public thief seldom escapes, for there are a thousand eyes watching every one, and anyone may discover theft and fraud and then no ministry has the power to protect the thief. But in Russia sometimes everyone knows of the thief, of the oppressor, of the one who perpetrates injustice for money; everyone knows, but all are silent because they are afraid. And the authorities themselves are silent, knowing that they themselves have sins, and all are concerned for only one thing: that the minister and the Tsar do not find out. And the Tsar is far away, Sire, just as God is high! * In Russia it is difficult and almost impossible for the bureaucrat not to be a thief. In the first place, everyone around him is stealing; habit becomes nature, and what formerly caused indignation and seemed repugnant soon becomes natural, unavoidable, and necessary; second, because the subordinate must often pay an exaction in some form or other to his superior; and finally, because if one should even think of remaining an honest man, then both his colleagues and his superiors hate him. At first they spread it about that he is an eccentric, a savage, unsocial person; and if he does not correct himself, then, if you please, he is a liberal, a dangerous freethinker, and then they will not rest until they crush him completely and wipe him from the face of the earth. From the lower bureaucrats trained in such a school are made, in time, the higher ones, who in their turn and in the same manner train the rising generation. And thievery and injustice and oppression live and grow in Russia like a thousand-armed polyp that, slash and cut it as you will, never dies.

Fear alone is not effective against this all-consuming disease. It terrifies you and stops you for a time, but only for a short time. Man becomes accustomed to anything, even to fear. Vesuvius is surrounded by settlements, and the very spot where Herculaneum and Pompeii are buried is covered with living creatures. In Switzerland populous villages sometimes

* The Russian proverb is 'Do Tsaria daleko, do Boga vysoko" or "Tsar' daleko, a Bog vysoko."

are found under a cliff that is on the verge of falling, and everyone knows that any day, any hour it may come crashing down and that in its awful fall everything living under it will be turned into dust. Yet no one moves from this spot, taking solace in the thought that perhaps the cliff will not fall for a long time. And the Russian bureaucrats are like this, Sire! They know how terrible is your wrath and how severe are your punishments when news of any injustice, of any thievery reaches you. And all tremble merely at the thought of your wrath, and nevertheless they continue to steal and oppress and perpetrate injustice! In part because it is difficult to break with an old ingrained habit; in part because everyone is sucked in, enmeshed and bound by other thieves who have stolen and are stealing with him. But most of all it is because everyone consoles himself with the thought that he will act so carefully and that he enjoys such powerful criminal protection that his sins will never reach your ear.

Fear alone is ineffective. Against such an evil other specifics are needed: nobility of feeling, independence of thought, the proud fearlessness of a clear conscience, respect for human worth in oneself and in others, and, finally, public contempt for all dishonorable, inhuman people, social shame, a social conscience! But these qualities, these forces, bloom only where there is free scope for the soul, not where slavery and fear prevail. These virtues are feared in Russia not because people might admire them but out of fear that free thoughts might come with them. . . .

I do not dare go into details, Sire! It would be laughable and impertinent for me to speak to you of what you yourself know a million times better than I. I know Russia but little, and what I have known of her I have told in my few articles and brochures and also in the letter of defense written by me in the Königstein Fortress.[76] I spoke in them often in insolent and criminal words against you, Sire; in a morbidly delirious spirit and tone, sinning against the Russian proverb "Don't carry the sweepings out of your hut." * But this was in keeping with

* Or "Don't wash dirty linen in public": "Iz izby soru ne vynosit'."

my convictions at the time, so that everything false and incor-
rect in them can be attributed to my ignorance of Russia, to
my feeble intelligence, and not to my heart.

I was struck and troubled most of all by the unhappy situation in which the so-called black people,* the good Russian
muzhik who is oppressed by everyone, now live. I felt greater
sympathy for him than for the other classes, incomparably
more than for the characterless and profligate Russian nobility.
I based all hopes for a rebirth, all faith in the great future of
Russia, on him. I saw in him freshness, an expansive soul, a
lucid intelligence not infected by foreign corruption, and Russian strength. And I thought: What might these people be if
they were given freedom and property, if they were taught to
read and write! And I asked: Why does the present government—autocratic, armed with boundless power, not limited
by statute or in fact by any outside law or any competing
power—why does it not use its omnipotence for the liberation,
elevation, and enlightenment of the Russian people? And
many other questions related to this main, basic one arose in
my soul! And instead of answering them as follows—as every
subject of Your Imperial Majesty should answer such doubts:
"It is no business of mine to judge these matters, the sovereign and his officials have knowledge of them; my duty is to
obey." Or instead of giving another answer, which is likewise
not devoid of basis in fact and which serves as a basis for the
first: The government looks at all problems from above, em-
bracing them all at the same time; I, however, look at them
from below and cannot see all the obstacles, all the difficulties,
the details and current conditions of internal as well as external policy; therefore I cannot determine the appropriate moment for every act.† Instead of these answers, I answered inso-
lently and seditiously in my mind and in my writings: "The
government does not free the Russian people, first, because
with all its omnipotent power, not limited by law, it is in fact

* Members of the unprivileged classes in old Russia. In modern parlance a
"black worker" is an unskilled worker, one who performs heavy, unpleasant
labor.
† Nicholas' marginal note: "NB" (according to Polonskii; not in Steklov).

limited by a multitude of circumstances, it is bound in invisible ways, it is bound by its corrupt administration, and finally it is bound by the egotism of the nobility. And even more, because it actually does not want freedom for or the enlightenment or elevation of the Russian people, seeing in them merely a soulless machine for its conquests in Europe!" This answer, completely antithetical to my duty as a faithful subject, did not contradict my democratic concepts.*

You might ask me: What do you think now? Sire! It will be difficult for me to answer this question! During the course of more than two years of solitary confinement I was able to rethink many things, and I can say that never in my life did I think so seriously as during this time. I was alone, far from all delusions, and I had been taught by living, bitter experience. I came to doubt the truth of many of my old thoughts even more when, entering Russia, I found here such a humane, noble, and sympathetic reception, instead of the crude and brutal treatment I expected. On the way, I heard much that I had not formerly known and which I never would have believed when abroad. Much, very much, changed in me. But can I say in good conscience that many, many traces of my old illness did not remain? One truth I comprehended perfectly: The science of government and the business of government are so great, so difficult, that few untrained minds are capable of comprehending them, not having been prepared by special education, a special atmosphere, and a close acquaintance and continual dealing with them. I comprehended that in the life of states and peoples there are many higher conditions and laws that are not subject to ordinary standards, and much that seems unjust, distressing, and brutal to us in private life becomes necessary in the higher political sphere. I realized that history has a mysterious movement of its own. This movement is logical, although it is often at variance with the logic of the world; it is salutary, although it does not always correspond to our personal wishes. I also comprehended that with few exceptions—very rare in history and, as it were, permitted by Provi-

---

* Nicholas' marginal note: "NB" (according to Polonskii; not in Steklov).

dence and sanctified by the acceptance of posterity—not a single private individual, no matter how sincere, true, or holy his
convictions seem, is called upon or has the right to raise a
seditious thought and an impotent hand against an inscrutable
higher destiny. I came to understand, in a word, that my own
projects and actions were to the highest degree laughable,
senseless, insolent, and criminal. They were criminal in respect to you, my sovereign, criminal in respect to Russia, my
fatherland, criminal in respect to all political and moral, divine
and human laws! But I shall return to my seditious, democratic
questions.

I also asked myself: "What benefit is there for Russia in her
conquests? And if half the world should be subjected to her,
will she then be happier, freer, richer? Will she even be more
powerful? Will the mighty Russian Tsardom not collapse? Now
so vast, almost boundless, will it not finally collapse when its
borders are extended still farther? What is the final goal of its
expansion? What will the Russian Tsardom give to the enslaved peoples in place of the independence of which they have
been robbed? There is no point in even speaking of freedom,
enlightenment, and national prosperity; perhaps it will give
them its total national character, oppressed by slavery! But
must and can the Russian or, more accurately, the Great Russian total national character be that of the entire world? Can
Western Europe ever become Russian in language, soul, and
heart? Can even all the Slav nations become Russian? Can they
forget their language—which even Little Russia has not yet
been able to forget—their literature, their native culture, in a
word, their own hearth, in order to disappear completely and,
in the words of Pushkin, 'mingle in the Russian sea'? [77] What
will they gain, what will Russia herself gain through such a
forced merging? They will gain the very same thing that Belorussia gained as a result of its long subjection to Poland:
complete exhaustion and stupefaction of the people. And Russia? Russia must carry on her shoulders all the weight of this
immense, complex, forced centralization. Russia will become
abhorrent to all other Slavs as she is now abhorrent to the
Poles. She will be not a liberator but an oppressor of her own

Slav family, their enemy against her will, at the expense of her own prosperity and at the expense of her own freedom. And in the end, hated by all, she will hate herself, finding in her forced victories nothing but suffering and slavery. In killing Slavs she will kill herself! Must this be the end of Slav life and Slav history, which are just beginning?"

Sire! I have not tried to soften my words! I have presented to you, in all their raw nakedness, questions that troubled my soul at that time, relying on your gracious indulgence and in order to explain to Your Imperial Majesty, if only a little, the way in which I, going or, better, staggering from question to question, from conclusion to conclusion, was able to convince myself in part of the necessity and morality of a Russian revolution.

I have said enough to show how great was the unbridled nature of my thoughts. But now, at the risk of sinning against logic and continuity, I hasten to skip a large number of similar questions and thoughts that brought me to my final revolutionary conclusion. It is difficult, Sire, and incredibly painful for me to speak to you of these subjects. Difficult because I do not know how I should explain myself. If I soften my words, then you may think that I wish to hide or minimize the insolence of my thoughts and that my confession is not sincere or complete. If, however, I repeat the expressions I used at the height of my political madness, then you very likely will think, Sire, that I—God preserve me—wish to flaunt my freethinking before you. Moreover, enumerating at length all my old thoughts, I should have to differentiate between those I have completely discarded and those I have partly or entirely preserved; I should have to go into endless explanations and discourses that would be not only improper here but completely repugnant to the spirit and the sole aim of this confession, which should contain only a simple and unhypocritical account of all my sins. But it is not so difficult as it is painful, Sire, for me to speak to you of what I dared think concerning the direction and spirit of your rule. It is painful in all respects: painful because of my position, for I stand before you, my sovereign, as a convicted criminal. It is painful to my pride: I can hear you, Sire, saying, "The boy is babbling of something about which he knows nothing!" And it is most painful of all to my heart, for I stand before you as a prodigal, alienated, depraved son before his outraged and wrathful father! *

In a word, Sire, I assured myself that Russia—in order to save her honor and her future—must carry out a revolution, overthrow your Tsarist authority, destroy monarchical rule, and, having thus liberated herself from internal slavery, take her place at the head of the Slav movement. Then she must turn her arms against the Emperor of Austria, against the Prussian King, against the Turkish Sultan, and also, if necessary, against both Germany and the Magyars—in a word, against the whole world— for the final liberation of all Slav nations from an alien yoke. Half of Prussian Silesia, the great part of West and of East Prussia—in a word, all Slavic-speaking, Polish-speaking lands—had to be detached from Germany. My fantasies went even further. I thought, I hoped that the Magyar nation (forced by circumstances, by its isolated position in the midst of Slav peoples, and also by its more Eastern than Western nature), that all the Moldavians and the Vlachs, and finally even Greece would enter the Slav union; and thus there would be created a single, free, Eastern state, a reborn Eastern world, as it were, in contrast to the Western, although not hostile to the latter, and that its capital would be Constantinople.

This is how far my revolutionary expectations had gone! Not my own ambitious plans, however, I swear to you, Sire, and I dare hope that you yourself will soon be convinced of this. But first I must answer the question: What form of government did I wish for Russia? [79] It will be very difficult for me to answer this, since my thoughts on this score were unclear and ill defined. Having lived eight years abroad, I knew that I did not know Russia, and I said to myself that it was not for me, all the more since I was outside Russia, to determine the laws and forms of her new existence. I saw that even in Western

* Nicholas' marginal note: "There is no cause for him to fear; I always forgive from the bottom of my heart anything directed against me personally!" [78]

Europe, where the conditions of life are already rather clearly defined, where there is incomparably more self-awareness than in Russia—I saw that even there no one was capable of foreseeing not only the constant forms of the future but even changes of the next day. And I said to myself: No one knows Russia now, neither Europeans nor Russians, because Russia is silent; and she is silent not because there is nothing for her to say but only because her tongue and all her movements are constrained. Let her but arise and speak and then we will learn both what she is thinking and what she wants; she herself will show us what forms and what institutions she needs. Had there then been with me even one Russian with whom I could have talked of Russia, then, I do not say that better or more reasonable concepts, but at least more definite ones would probably have taken shape in my mind. But I was completely alone with my plans, and thousands of vague, mutually contradictory fantasies jostled one another in my mind. I could not put them in order, and, convinced of the impossibility of escaping from this labyrinth by my own strength alone, I postponed the solution of all problems until I should be on Russian soil.

I wanted a republic. But what kind of republic? Not a parliamentary one. Representative rule, constitutional forms, a parliamentary aristocracy, and the so-called balance of powers in which all active forces are so cunningly distributed that not one of them can act; in a word, all that narrow, cunningly woven, and weak-willed political catechism of the Western liberals never was the object of my adoration, of my sincere interest, or even of my respect.[80] And at this time I had begun to disdain it even more, seeing the fruits of parliamentary forms in France, in Germany, and even in the Slav Congress, especially in the Polish section, where the Poles also played at parliament, just as the Germans played at revolution. Moreover, a Russian parliament, and a Polish one too, would be constituted only of the gentry; in the Russian one the merchants might also enter, but the huge mass of the people, the real people, the bulwark and strength of Russia, in which is contained her life and all her future—the people, I thought, would remain without representatives and would be oppressed and humiliated by that very same gentry which now humiliates them. I thought that in Russia more than anywhere else a strong dictatorial government that would be exclusively concerned with elevating and educating the popular masses would be necessary; a government free in the direction it takes and in its spirit, but without parliamentary forms; with the printing of books free in content but without the freedom of printing; surrounded by like minds, illuminated by their counsel, strengthened by their willing assistance, but not limited by anyone or anything. I told myself that the whole difference between such a dictatorship and a monarchical government would consist in this, that the former, because of the spirit in which it is established, must strive to make its existence unnecessary as soon as possible, having in view only the freedom, independence, and gradual maturing of the people; monarchical government, on the contrary, must endeavor to prevent its existence from ever becoming unnecessary, and therefore must maintain its subjects in unalterable childhood.[81]

What there would be after the dictatorship I did not know, and I thought that no one could now foresee this. And who would be dictator? You might think that I was preparing myself for this high position. But such a supposition would be definitely unjust. I must say, Sire, that except for exaltation—sometimes fanatic, but fanatic more as a result of circumstances and my unnatural situation than from my nature—there were in me none of those brilliant qualities or those powerful vices that produce either remarkable political figures or great state criminals. Both formerly and at this time there was in me so little ambition that I would willingly have subordinated myself to anyone if only I had seen in him ability and means and a firm will to serve those principles in which I then believed as absolute truth. I would have followed him joyously and would have subordinated myself zealously because I always loved and respected discipline when it was based on conviction and faith. I do not say that there was no pride in me, but it was never predominant in me; on the contrary, I had to gain control of myself and, as it were, disregard my nature when I was preparing to speak in public or even write for the public. There were not in me those tremendous vices à la Danton or à la Mirabeau,[82] that insatiable, vast depravity that is ready to turn the whole world upside down for its satisfaction. And if there was egotism in me, it consisted solely in a need for movement, in a need for activity. There was always a basic defect in my nature: a love for the fantastic, for unusual, unheard-of adventures, for undertakings that open up a boundless horizon and whose end no one can foresee. I would feel suffocated and nauseated in an ordinary calm milieu. People usually search for tranquillity and view it as the greatest good; it always led me to despair, however; my soul would be in unremitting agitation, demanding activity, movement, and life. I should have been born somewhere in the forests of America, among the Western colonists, there where civilization has scarcely dawned and where all life is a ceaseless struggle against wild men, wild nature, and not in an organized civil society. Also, had fate wished to make me a sailor from my youth, I even now would probably be a very respectable man; I would not have thought of politics and would have sought no other adventures and storms than those of the sea. But fate did not will either the one or the other, and my need for movement and activity remained unsatisfied. This need, subsequently united with democratic exaltation, was almost my only motive force. As far as the latter is concerned, it can be expressed in a few words: love of freedom and inevitable hatred for all oppression, even more when it fell on others than when it fell on myself. To look for my happiness in the happiness of others, for my own worth in the worth of all those around me, to be free in the freedom of others—that is my whole faith, the aspiration of my whole life. I considered it my sacred duty to rebel against all oppression, no matter where it came from or on whom it fell. There was always a lot of quixotism in me, not only political but also private. I could not view injustice—to say nothing of actual oppression—with equanimity. I often interfered in the affairs of others without being asked, and with no right, and without having given myself time to think it over; and thus throughout my very restless but empty and useless life I did many foolish things and brought upon myself many troubles and acquired several enemies, I myself hating almost no one. Here, Sire, is the true key to all my thoughtless acts, sins, and crimes. I speak of this with such assuredness and so positively because during the last two years I have had enough leisure to study myself, to think over all my past life; and now I look at myself dispassionately, as only one who is dying or even completely dead can look.

With such direction to my thoughts and feelings I could not think of myself as a dictator, I could not nurture ambitious designs in my soul. On the contrary, I was so convinced that I would perish in the unequal struggle that I even wrote several times to my friend Reichel that he and I had taken leave of each other for the last time; that if I did not perish in Germany, then I would perish in Poland, and if not in Poland, then in Russia. More than once I also said to the Germans and the Poles when they were arguing in my presence about the future forms of government: "We are called to destroy and not to build; others better, more intelligent, and fresher than we will build." I hoped for the same thing for Russia. I thought that new, strong people would emerge from the revolutionary movement and that they would take charge of it and lead it to its goal.

You might ask me: With such ill-defined thoughts, not knowing yourself what would come of your undertaking, how could you decide on such a terrible thing as a Russian revolution? Could it be that you had never heard of the Pugachev Rebellion? Or do you not know of what barbarity, of what bestial cruelty rebelling Russian muzhiks are capable? And do you not remember the words of Pushkin: "May God deliver us from a Russian rebellion, senseless and merciless"? [83]

Sire! It will be more painful for me to answer this question, this reproach, than it was for me to answer all the previous ones. More painful because, although my crime did not go beyond the realm of thought, in my thoughts I even then felt myself a criminal and shuddered at the possible consequences of my criminal undertaking—and did not give it up! True, I tried to deceive myself in the vain hope of the possibility of stopping, of curbing the drunken fury of the unbridled mob; but I had little hope and justified myself with the sophism that sometimes even a terrible evil is necessary, and finally I comforted myself with the thought that if there are to be many victims, then I too shall fall with them . . . and God knows! would I have had enough character, strength, and madness to begin—I do not say carry out—a criminal deed? God knows! I want to believe "No," but perhaps "Yes." What does fanaticism not do! And for good reason people say that in an evil undertaking only the first step is difficult. I thought much and long about this matter and even now do not know what to say, but I only thank God that he did not permit me to become a monster and the hangman of my fellow countrymen!

I also am unable to give a definite answer concerning the means and ways I thought to use for propaganda in Russia. I did not and could not have definite hopes, for I had no contact with Russia. But I was ready to seize on any means that presented itself to me: a conspiracy in the army, a mutiny of Russian soldiers, enticing Russian prisoners—if such were to be found—to form the nucleus of a Russian revolutionary army, and, finally, a peasant uprising. . . . In a word, Sire, there was neither limit nor measure to my crime in thought and intentions against your sacred authority! And once more I thank providence for stopping me in time and not permitting me to commit or even begin a single one of my disastrous ventures against you, my sovereign, or against my motherland. Nevertheless I know that it is not so much the act itself as the intent that makes the criminal, and—setting aside my German sins for which I was condemned at first to death and then to confinement for life in a workhouse—I fully and from the depths of my soul confess that most of all I am a criminal against you, Sire, a criminal against Russia, and that my crimes deserve the most severe punishment! *

The most painful part of my confession is finished. Now it remains for me to confess to you my German sins—true, more

---

* Nicholas' marginal note: "The sword does not sever the head that has acknowledged guilt, may God forgive him!" The first part of the Tsar's note is a Russian proverb: "Povinnuiu golovu i mech' ne sechet."

positive and not limited only to my thinking, but nevertheless lying incomparably lighter on my conscience than those sins in thought against you, Sire, and against Russia, whose detailed and unhypocritical description I have completed. I turn again to my narrative.

At that time I was searching for a fulcrum for my activities. Not finding one among the Poles, for all the reasons mentioned above, I began to look for one among the Slavs. Subsequently also convinced that I would find nothing even in the Slav Congress, I began to gather people outside the congress and was about to form a secret society, the first in which I had participated, a society named Slav Friends. Several Slovaks, Moravians, Croats, and Serbs joined it. Permit me, Sire, not to name them; it is enough that, except for me, not a single subject of Your Imperial Majesty participated in it and that the society existed but a few days, being dispersed, together with the Prague congress, by the uprising, by the victory of the troops, and by the forced departure of all the Slavs from the city of Prague. It did not even succeed in getting organized or even in laying the first bases for its activity, but was scattered to the four corners of the earth without having arranged for communications or correspondence, so that afterward I did not have nor could I have communication with a single one of its former members, and in my subsequent activities it had no influence. I have mentioned it only in order to omit nothing in my detailed account.[84]

The Slav Congress later changed its direction. In part yielding to pressure from the Poles, in part from my contribution, and also from the contribution of those Slavs who thought as I did, it began to move a bit in a spirit more all-Slav, more liberal (I do not say democratic), and ceased serving the special views of the Austrian government. This was its death sentence.[85] The Prague uprising, however, was brought about not by the congress but by students and the party of so-called Czech democrats. The latter were then still very few in number and seemed to have no definite political direction, and supported the rebellion because rebellions were then generally in vogue. At this time I was little acquainted with them, for they hardly attended the meetings of the congress at all, but remained for the most part outside Prague, in neighboring villages, where they incited the peasants to take part in the uprising they had prepared. I knew nothing of their plans or even of their intended movement, and was just as astonished by it as were all the other members of the Slav Congress. Not until the evening before the appointed day—and then only indefinitely and vaguely—did I first hear of the independent uprising of students and the working class, and with others tried to persuade the students to refrain from an impossible undertaking and not give the Austrian troops an opportunity for an easy victory. It was obvious that General Prince Windischgrätz wished for nothing so fervently as for such an opportunity to restore his soldiers' morale, which was low, and their military discipline, which was weakened, in order to give Europe, after so many shameful defeats, the first example of a victory of troops over the seditious masses. By his many measures, he seemed to want to irritate the inhabitants of Prague; he manifestly was challenging them to mutiny, and the stupid students with their unheard-of demands—which no general could carry out without disgracing himself before his entire army—presented him with his desired occasion to begin military operations.[86]

I remained in Prague until the capitulation, serving as a volunteer: I went from one barricade to another carrying a gun—I shot several times; but I was more like a guest in all this affair, not expecting great results from it. In the end, however, I advised the students and other participants to overthrow the Rathaus,* which was carrying on secret talks with Prince Windischgrätz, and to put in its place a military committee with dictatorial powers. They wanted to follow my advice, but it was too late; Prague capitulated, and early the next day I set out to return to Breslau, where this time I stayed, if I am not mistaken, until the early days of July.[87]

In describing the impression made on me by my first meeting with the Slavs in Prague, I said that there awakened

* Town hall.

within me then a Slav heart and new Slav feelings that almost caused me to forget all interests tying me to the democratic movement of Western Europe. The senseless cry raised by the Germans against the Slavs following the dissolution of the Slav Congress, coming from all sides of Germany, and most of all from the Frankfurt National Assembly, affected me even more strongly.[88] Now this was not a democratic cry but a cry of German egotism. The Germans wanted freedom for themselves, not for others. Gathering in Frankfurt, they really thought that they had become a united and powerful nation and that now it was up to them to decide the fate of the world! *Das deutsche Vaterland,* which previously existed only in their songs and in conversations over tobacco and beer, was to become the fatherland of half of Europe. The Frankfurt Assembly, which itself came out of a rebellion, was based on rebellion, and existed only through rebellion, began to call the Italians and the Poles rebels and to look upon them as seditious and criminal enemies of German grandeur and German omnipotence! * It called the German war for Schleswig-Holstein, *stammverwandt und meerumschlungen,*† a holy war, and it called the war of the Italians for the freedom of Italy and the undertakings of the Poles in the Duchy of Poznań criminal! But German national fury was turned even more strongly against the Austrian Slavs who had gathered in Prague. Since ancient times the Germans had been accustomed to view them as their serfs and did not want to permit them even to breathe in Slavic! In this hatred for the Slavs, in these Slav-devouring cries, absolutely all the German parties participated. Not only did the conservatives and the liberals shout against the Slavs, as they did against Italy and Poland, but the democrats too shouted louder than the others: in newspapers, in brochures, in legislative and national assemblies, in clubs, in beer halls, on the street . . . It was such a din, such a furious storm, that if a German shout could have killed or harmed anyone, then all the Slavs would long since have died. Before my journey to Prague I enjoyed great esteem among the Breslau democrats,

---

* Nicholas' marginal note: "Beautiful!"

† Of one blood and embraced by the sea.

but all my influence was lost and turned to naught when, on returning, I began to defend the rights of Slavs in a democratic club; everyone suddenly began to shout at me and did not even let me finish speaking, and this was my last effort at oratory in the Breslau club and, in general, in all German clubs and public gatherings.* [89] The Germans suddenly had become loathsome to me, so loathsome that I could not speak with one of them with equanimity, could not bear to hear the German language or a German voice, and I remember that once when a little German beggar boy walked up to me to ask for alms, I could hardly refrain from giving him a thrashing.

Not only I but all Slavs, by no means excluding the Poles, felt this way. The Poles had been deceived by the French revolutionary government, deceived by Germans, insulted by German Jews. The Poles began to say loudly that only one thing was left to them: to resort to the protection of the Russian Emperor and to beg of him as a favor the annexation of all the Polish, Austrian, and Prussian provinces to Russia. Such was the general opinion in the Duchy of Poznań, in Galicia, and in Kraków; only the emigration disagreed, but at this time the emigration was almost without influence. One might have thought that the Poles were being hypocritical and merely wanted to frighten the Germans; but they did not speak of this to the Germans, only among themselves, and they spoke with such passion and used such expressions that even then I could not doubt their sincerity and I am now still convinced that if you, Sire, had wished at that time to raise the Slav banner, then they unconditionally, without discussion, blindly submitting to your will, they and all others who speak Slavic in the Austrian and Prussian possessions would have thrown themselves with joy and fanaticism under the broad wings of the Russian eagle and would have rushed with fury not only against the hated Germans but against all Western Europe as well.†

A strange thought was then born within me. I suddenly

---

* Nicholas' marginal note: "About time!"

† Nicholas' marginal note: "I don't doubt it; i.e., I would have stood at the head of the revolution as a Slav Masaniello; thank you!" [90]

took it into my head to write to you, Sire, and was on the point of starting the letter. It too contained a sort of confession, more vain, more high-flown than the one I am now writing *—I was then at liberty and had not yet learned from experience—but it was quite sincere and heartfelt: I confessed my sins; I prayed for forgiveness; then, having made a rather drawn-out and pompous review of the current situation of the Slav peoples, I implored you, Sire, in the name of all oppressed Slavs, to come to their aid, to take them under your mighty protection, to be their savior, their father, and, having proclaimed yourself Tsar of all the Slavs, finally to raise the Slav banner in eastern Europe to the terror of the Germans and all other oppressors and enemies of the Slav race! The letter was very complex and long, fantastic, rash, but written with passion and from the soul. It contained much that was ludicrous, absurd, but also much that was true; in a word, it was a faithful depiction of my spiritual disarray and of those countless contradictions that then troubled my mind. I tore up this letter and burned it without having finished it. I came to my senses and thought that it would seem unusually ludicrous and insolent to you, Sire, that I, a subject of Your Imperial Majesty—and not even an ordinary subject but a state criminal—would dare write to you, and write not limiting myself to a plea for pardon but daring to offer you counsel, trying to persuade you to change your policy! I told myself that my letter, which would be of no use whatsoever, would only compromise me in the eyes of the democrats who by chance might learn of my unsuccessful, strange, and not at all democratic attempt. The following two circumstances, which I encountered in a strange manner at one and the same time, more than any other reasons forced me to renounce this intention.

First, I learned (I may say from an official source, namely, from the chief of police in Breslau) † that the Russian government had demanded my extradition from the Prussian, basing themselves on the fact that allegedly I with the aforementioned Poles—two brothers whose surnames I had never heard before

* Nicholas' marginal note: "Too bad he did not send it!"
† His name was Kuh, according to Steklov.

and now do not remember—intended to make an attempt on the life of Your Imperial Majesty.[91] I have already answered this slander, and I implore you, Sire, permit me not to refer to it further! Second, the rumor of my espionage was not limited to the stupid, idle talk of the Poles, but found a place in German journals. Dr. Marx, one of the leaders of the German communists in Brussels, who had come to hate me more than others because I did not wish to be forced to attend their societies and meetings, was at this time the editor of the *Rheinische Zeitung,** which came out in Cologne. He was the first to print the correspondence from Paris in which I was reproached for having caused the death of many Poles by my denunciations; and since the *Rheinische Zeitung* was the favorite reading of the German democrats, everyone everywhere suddenly began to speak loudly of my supposed treachery.[92] I was pressed from both sides: in the eyes of the governments I was a miscreant planning regicide, whereas in the eyes of the public I was a foul spy. I was then convinced that both calumnious rumors came from one and the same source. They irrevocably decided my fate: I vowed in my soul that I would not abandon my enterprises and would not be diverted from a path once begun and would go forward without looking back, and would go until I perished, and that in perishing I would prove to the Poles and the Germans that I was not a traitor.

After several explanations (some written and personal, some printed in German journals),[93] finding no more use or purpose in staying in Breslau, I set out at the beginning of July for Berlin and remained there until the end of September.† In Berlin I often saw the French minister, Emmanuel Arago; at his home I met the Turkish minister, who repeatedly asked me to visit him, but I did not, not wishing it to be said of me that I served Turkish policy against Russia in any way whatsoever, when on the contrary I desired the liberation of the Slavs from Turkish rule and the complete destruction of the latter. I also saw many German and Polish members of the Prussian legis-

* Actually *Neue Rheinische Zeitung.*
† Nicholas' marginal note: "NB."

lative or constituent assembly, the majority of them democrats; I kept a great distance from all of them, however, even from those with whom I had formerly been rather close in Breslau. It always seemed to me that people were looking at me as at a spy, and I was ready to hate everyone for this and I shunned them all.[94] Never, Sire, was it so difficult for me as at this time; neither before nor afterward, or even when, deprived of freedom, I was obliged to pass through all the ordeals of two criminal trials. Here I understood how terrible the position of a real spy must be, or how base a real spy must be to bear his existence with equanimity. It was very painful for me, Sire!

Moreover, the European horizon had visibly darkened for me, a democrat. After the revolution, reaction or preparations for reaction were following everywhere. The June events in Paris had awful consequences for all democrats, not only in Paris, in France, but in all Europe.[95] In Germany there were as yet no obvious reactionary measures, and it seemed that everyone was enjoying complete freedom; but those who had eyes could see that the governments were quietly preparing, counseling with one another, collecting their forces, and only waiting for a convenient moment to deliver a decisive blow, and that they were tolerating the muddleheaded chatter of the German parliaments only because their expectation of benefit from them was even greater than their fear of harmful consequences. They were not disappointed: the German liberals and democrats killed themselves and made the victory of the governments very easy. The Slav question at this time had also become confused: Ban Jelačić's war in Hungary seemed to be a Slav war, was undertaken supposedly only to defend the Slovaks and South Slavs from the unbearable claims of the Magyars; in essence, however, this war was the beginning of the Austrian reaction. I was in grave doubt, not knowing with whom to sympathize. I definitely did not trust Jelačić, but at this time even Kossuth was still a bad democrat; he was flirting with the reactionary Frankfurt Assembly and was even ready to make peace with Innsbruck and serve it against

Vienna and against the Poles and against Italy only if the Innsbruck court was willing to agree to his special Hungarian demands.

During all of this, I was pinned down in Berlin by lack of
money. If I had had money,* then I could have gone to
Hungary to be an eyewitness, and many pages would then
have been added to this already many-paged confession! But I
had no money and I could not stir from the spot. Also there
were no contacts with the Slavs; † except for one insignificant
letter from L'udovít Štúr, to which I wanted to reply but could
not, for I did not know his address, I did not receive a line
from Austria and did not write to anyone.[96] In a word, until
the very month of December I remained in complete inactivity, so that I do not even know what to say about that time except that I waited by the sea for the weather,‡ firmly intending
to seize the first opportunity for action. In what spirit I wanted
to act, you already know, Sire! This was a most difficult time
for me. Without money, without friends, proclaimed a spy,
alone in the midst of a populous city, I did not know what to
do, what to undertake, and sometimes did not even know on
what and how I would live the next day. Not only by lack of
money was I tied down; I was also pinned down to Berlin, to
Prussia, and generally to northern Germany by calumnious
rumors spread at my expense; and although the political circumstances had already visibly changed and were of such a
nature that I had almost completely ceased to expect and to
hope, I could not and did not want to return to Paris—the sole
refuge that remained to me—without first proving in living
deed the sincerity of my democratic convictions. I had to endure to the end in order to redeem my sullied honor. I became
bitter, antisocial, I became a fanatic, I was ready for any undertaking, however difficult,§ as long as it was not base; and

* Nicholas' marginal note: "NB" (according to Polonskii; not in Steklov).

† Nicholas' marginal note: "NB" (according to Polonskii; not in Steklov).

‡ A Russian saying that means to wait with little hope for things to im-
prove.

§ Nicholas' marginal note: "NB."

all of me was changed, as it were, into the revolutionary idea and the passion for destruction.

At the end of September, probably at the demand of the Russian embassy (without, however, my having given the slightest cause for it), I was forced to leave Berlin.[97] I returned to Breslau, but at the beginning of October I was forced * to leave Breslau † and, generally speaking, all the Prussian possessions, with the threat that if I returned I would be handed over to the Russian government. After such a threat, of course I did not even try to return. I wanted to stay in Dresden, but I was expelled from there too because of a misunderstanding, as the minister later said, and on the basis of an old demand of the Russian embassy. Thus, hounded from place to place, I finally settled in the principality of Anhalt-Köthen,‡ which, located in the midst of the Prussian possessions, strangely enough enjoyed at that time the freest constitution not only in Germany but, I think, in the whole world, and had become as a consequence, although not for long, a refuge for political exiles.[98] In Köthen I found several old acquaintances with whom I had studied at the University of Berlin. There were also a legislative assembly and popular assemblies there, and a club and *Ständchen* and *Katzenmusik*, § but in essence almost no one engaged in politics. Thus, until the middle of November, my acquaintances and I knew almost no other occupations than hunting for rabbits and other wild game. This was a time of rest for me.

My rest did not last long. Fate was preparing for me a tomb-like rest: imprisonment in a fortress. Even in October, when Ban Jelačić, bypassing Pest, moved directly on Vienna,[99] and

---

* Nicholas' marginal note: "NB" (according to Polonskii; not in Steklov).

† Bakunin's note: "In Breslau, as well as in Berlin, the democrats were about to prepare for armed resistance to the first reactionary measures of the Prussian government. Perhaps Prussian Silesia was never so ready for a general popular uprising as it was precisely at this time. I saw these preparations, rejoiced in them, but did not participate in them, anticipating more decisive circumstances."

‡ Nicholas' marginal note: "NB."

§ *Ständchen*, serenade; *Katzenmusik*, caterwauling.

General Prince Windischgrätz and his troops left Prague, I wanted to go to the latter city, desiring to incite the Czech democrats to a second uprising.* I thought better of it, however, and remained in Köthen. I thought better of it because I did not yet have connections with Prague, and I did not know what changes might have taken place there after the June days and what the trend of thought was at the time. I was poorly acquainted with the democrats and I did not hope for success, but, on the contrary, expected strong opposition from Palacký's Czech constitutional party. In Prague they had long since forgotten me, I thought, and partly to remind the Prague inhabitants of me and as far as possible to give the Slav movement another direction more consonant with my own Slav and democratic expectations, and partly to prove to the Poles and Germans that I was not a Russian spy and to pave the way for a rapprochement with them, I began to write an appeal to the Slavs, *Aufruf an die Slaven,* which was later published in Leipzig.[100] It is also to be found among the documents of indictment. I worked on it for a long time, more than a month. I put it off, then took it up again, changed it several times, and for a long time could not bring myself to print it. I could not express my Slav idea in it straightforwardly and clearly because I wanted to draw close to the German democrats again, considering this rapprochement necessary, and I had to tack between the Slavs and the Germans—a type of sailing for which I had no great ability or experience and even less liking. I wished to convince the Slavs of the necessity of a rapprochement with the German as well as the Magyar democrats. Conditions were no longer as they had been in May: the revolution had weakened, reaction had everywhere become stronger, and only through the united forces of all the European democracies could one hope to defeat the reactionary league of rulers.

In November, following the Vienna events, the Prussian Constituent Assembly was dissolved, also in a violent manner. As a consequence several former deputies gathered in Köthen,

* Nicholas' marginal note: "NB" (according to Polonskii; not in Steklov).

among others Hexamer and d'Ester,[101] members of the central committee of all democratic clubs in Germany. This committee was not secret, however, having been chosen not long before in public meetings of the democratic congress in Berlin. But it soon began to organize secret societies all over Germany, and one may say that the German secret societies began only at this time. Without any doubt some had existed before, namely communist ones, but they definitely had remained without any influence. Before November everything was done publicly in Germany—plots and revolts and preparations for revolts— and anyone who wanted to could know of them. For a long time the Germans, spoiled by a revolution that had fallen from the sky, as it were, without any effort on their part and almost without bloodshed, could not be convinced of the governments' growing strength and their own weakness; they chattered, sang, drank, were terrible in word and children in deed, and thought there would be no end to their freedom, and that they needed merely to frown a little to set all the governments atremble. The happenings in Vienna and Berlin taught them the opposite, however; here they realized that to keep their easily won freedom they would have to take more serious measures, and all Germany began secretly to prepare for a new revolution.

I saw d'Ester and Hexamer for the first time in Berlin, but I was then still not well acquainted with them, for I shunned them just as I did all other people, Germans and Poles. In Köthen I became more closely acquainted with them; at first they did not trust me, thinking that I was indeed a spy; later, however, they came to trust me. I talked and argued with them a great deal about the Slav question; for a long time I could not convince them of the necessity for the Germans to renounce all claims to Slav lands; finally I was able to convince them of this. Thus our political relations began—the first positive relations with a definite goal that I had with Germans, and in general with any active political party whatsoever. They promised me to use all their influence with the German democrats to root out from them hatred for and prejudice against the Slavs; and I promised them to act in the same spirit with the latter. Our mutual obligations were limited to this at first. Since they no longer feared me, I knew of their intentions, preparations, of the formation of secret societies, I also heard of the relations with foreign democrats that had just then been initiated; but I definitely did not interfere in their affairs and did not even want to ask, fearing to arouse new suspicions. But I hastened to complete the *Appeal to the Slavs,* which I printed in Leipzig soon afterward.

At the end of December—partly to be nearer Bohemia and live in a city offering more means than Köthen of contact with all points, and partly because I had heard that the Prussian government intended to detain all who had fled there—I, with Hexamer and d'Ester, moved to Leipzig.[102] There by chance I became acquainted with several young Slavs whose names and characters are set forth in detail in the Austrian documents of indictment. Among them were two brothers, Gustav and Adolf Straka,[103] Czechs who were then studying theology at the University of Leipzig. They were both good and noble young men who did not think of politics before their acquaintance with me, although they were both zealous Slavs, and their ruin, caused by me alone, is a great sin on my soul. Before my arrival in Leipzig they were of an opinion completely opposite to mine: they were great admirers of Jelačić. To their misfortune I met them, enticed them, changed their way of thinking, tore them away from peaceful pursuits, and persuaded them to be instruments of my undertakings in Bohemia. And now if I could alleviate their lot by the worsening of my own, I would gladly take their punishment on myself. But all this is too late! Aside from them, however, there was not on my soul, formerly or at this time or later, a single person whom I had enticed. For them only must I answer to God.

It was precisely through them that I learned that my *Appeal to the Slavs* had received a strong sympathetic response in Prague; that an excerpt from it had even been translated and printed in one of the Czech democratic journals, whose editor was Dr. Sabina.[104] This gave rise in me to the thought of summoning several Czechs and a few Poles to Leipzig for a conference and for an understanding with the Germans, with the goal of laying the first foundation for common revolutionary action. Consequently, I sent Gustav Straka to Prague with a message to Arnold—also an editor of a Czech democratic newspaper [105]—and to Sabina.* At that time I knew only their names, not yet being personally acquainted with them. [107] I also wrote to those of my Polish acquaintances in the Duchy of Poznań, from whom I could expect more sympathy and cooperation than from others. But absolutely not one of the Poles came, no one even answered me; and from Prague there came only Arnold, who had not permitted Straka to invite Sabina too—in part because he did not trust him, and in part, I think, because of petty jealousy. All these circumstances—divulged not by me, however, but by Arnold himself and by the Straka brothers—are set forth in detail in the Austrian acts of indictment. I shall not enter, Sire, into the petty details necessary in an inquisitorial investigation for the discovery of truth, but which are unnecessary and irrelevant in freely given and simplehearted confession. I shall mention in the course of this narrative only those circumstances that are necessary for continuity or those essential facts that are unknown to both investigating commissions.

Setting about to describe the last act of my unhappy revolutionary career, I must first say what I desired; then I shall describe my activities.

My political fever,irritated and excited by previous failures, by the intolerable nature of my strange situation, and finally by the victory of reaction in Europe, reached its greatest paroxysm at this time: I was completely transmuted into revolutionary desire, into a thirst for revolution, and was, I think, among all red republicans and democrats the reddest. My plan was the following.

The German democrats were preparing a general uprising of Germany for the spring of 1849. I wanted the Slavs to unite with them as well as with the Magyars, who were then already in open and decisive revolt against the Austrian Emperor. I

* Bakunin's note: "I must note here that I also sent with Gustav Straka an address to the Slav Linden Society, a more or less democratic Czech club, [106] but that Sabina himself retained it, finding it too dangerous."

wanted them to unite with both the Germans and the Magyars, not in order to merge with Germany or submit to the Magyars, but in order that with the victory of revolution in Europe, the independence of the Slav peoples should also be affirmed. Now the time seemed ripe for such an understanding; the Magyars and the Germans, having learned from experience and needing allies, were prepared to renounce their former claims. I hoped that the Poles would agree to be mediators between Kossuth and the Hungarian Slavs, and I wanted to take on myself mediation between the Slavs and the Germans. I wanted the center and head of this new Slav movement to be Bohemia and not Poland. I wanted this for many reasons: first, because all of Poland was so exhausted and demoralized by previous defeats that I did not believe in the possibility of her liberation without foreign assistance; whereas Bohemia, still almost untouched by the reaction, was then enjoying complete freedom, was strong, fresh, and contained all necessary resources for a successful revolutionary movement. Moreover, I did not want the Poles to stand at the head of the intended revolution, fearing that they would either give it a narrow, exclusively Polish character or possibly, if it seemed necessary to them, betray the other Slavs to their old allies the Western European democrats or, even more easily, to the Magyars. Finally, I knew that Prague is a capital, as it were (a sort of Moscow), for all Austrian, non-Polish Slavs; [108] and I hoped, I think not without basis, that if Prague were to rise, then all the other Slav peoples would follow her example and be carried away by her movement—in defiance of Jelačić and the other adherents of the Austrian dynasty, on the whole not so numerous. And so from the Germans I expected agreement, sympathy, and if necessary also armed assistance against the Prussian government, which, attracted by the Russian example and fearing contagion, most likely would not wish to be an idle witness to the revolutionary conflagration in Bohemia. From the Poles I expected mediation with the Magyars, collaboration, officers, and, most of all, money, which I did not have and without which any undertaking would be impossible. But my main expectations and hopes were concentrated on Bohemia.

I relied on the Bohemian, Czech, and German peasants even more than on Prague and on city dwellers in general. The great mistake of the Germans, and at first also of the French democrats, was, in my opinion, that their propaganda was limited to the cities and did not penetrate to the villages; the cities, one might say, had become aristocrats, and consequently the villages not only remained indifferent onlookers of the revolution but in many places even began to evince a hostile disposition toward it. But it seemed that nothing would be easier than to incite a revolutionary spirit in the agricultural class, especially in Germany, where so many remnants of the ancient feudal order still existed, depressing the land, not excluding Prussia itself, which, with general liberty of property and person, preserved in some provinces—for example, Silesia—traces of former subjection,* and in which alongside a rather numerous class of freeholders there exists an even more numerous class of poor peasants, the so-called *Häusler,*† and even completely homeless people. But nowhere was the agricultural class so inclined toward the revolutionary movement as in Bohemia. In Bohemia until 1848, feudalism still existed in its entirety, with all its burdens and oppressions: the lords' law courts, feudal taxes and dues, tithes and other religious obligations depressed the property of the well-to-do peasants. The propertyless class was even more numerous, and its situation was more onerous than in Germany itself. Moreover, in Bohemia there are many factories and hence many factory workers, and factory workers are, as it were, summoned by fate to be recruits of democratic propaganda.

In the year 1848 all oppression, all objects of eternal dissatisfaction and complaints of the peasants, all the old taxes, complex obligations, and work ceased; they ceased, together with the decrepit life of the political organism of the Austrian mon-

* Bakunin uses the word *poddanstvo,* citizenship, status of a citizen. Steklov notes that he means "serfdom."
† Cottagers.

archy. But they only ceased, they were not destroyed. After oppression followed anarchy. The government—frightened, completely flustered, and boldly grasping for anything that might save it from going under completely—recalled its democratic ruse of 1846 in Galicia and suddenly proclaimed, without any preliminary measures, unlimited and unconditional freedom of landownership and of the peasants. Its agents covered the Bohemian land, preaching the goodness of the government. But in Bohemia relationships were not at all the same as in Galicia. In Bohemia the oppressing and hated class of rich landowners, the gentry, the aristocracy, consists not of Polish conspirators but of Germans, devoted body and soul to the Austrian dynasty, devoted even more to the old Austrian order of things, which is so advantageous to them. The people stopped going out to work on the master's land, neither did they want to pay any duties except governmental ones, and these they paid reluctantly, quite unwillingly. The landowning class—the gentry, the aristocracy; in a word, all who make up the Austrian party proper in Bohemia—became impoverished and weakened; and with all this the government gained nothing because the people who had always willingly followed the teachings of the Czech patriots did not evince for it any particular love or gratitude for the great gift of freedom, which was not made in time. On the contrary, they did not trust the government, hearing that it was under the influence of the aristocracy, and constantly fearing that it would take it into its head to return the people anew to their old subjection. Finally, unusual levies of new recruits, repeated several times in the course of one year, aroused general grumbling and absolute displeasure among the Bohemian people. In such a mood *it was easy to move them to an uprising.*

I hoped for a decisive, radical revolution in Bohemia; in a word, one that, even if it were subsequently defeated, succeeded in so overturning everything and turning everything upside down that the Austrian government after its victory would not find a single thing in its old place. Taking advan-

* Italicized according to Polonskii; not in Steklov.

tage of the fortunate circumstance that all the gentry in Bohemia—and, in general, the whole class of rich landowners—consisted exclusively of Germans, I wanted to drive out all the gentry, all the hostilely inclined clergy, and, having indiscriminately confiscated all the landed property of the masters, divide part of it among the poor peasants to encourage them to join the revolution, and turn part of it into a source of extraordinary revenue for the revolution. I wanted to destroy all castles, burn absolutely all documents throughout the whole of Bohemia, all administrative as well as judicial, governmental, and manorial papers and documents, and declare all hypothecs paid, as well as all other debts not exceeding a certain sum (for example, 1,000 or 2,000 gulden). In a word, the revolution that I was planning was terrible, unparalleled, although it was directed more against things than against people.[109] It would really have so overturned everything, it would have so eaten into the blood and the life of the people that even if victorious the Austrian government would never have had the strength to root it out. It would not have known how to begin, what to do; it could not have collected or even found the remnants of the old order, which had been destroyed forever, and it never could have made peace with the Bohemian people. Such a revolution, not limited to one nationality, would have attracted by its example, by its fiery red propaganda, not only Moravia and Austrian Silesia but also Prussian Silesia and, in general, all the German borderlands, so that the German revolution itself—until this time a revolution of cities, burghers, factory workers, littérateurs, and lawyers—would have been turned into a general revolution.

But my plans were not limited to this. I wanted to transform all Bohemia into a revolutionary camp, to create in it a force capable not only of protecting the revolution within the country itself but also of acting offensively outside of Bohemia, at the same time inciting all the Slav nations, summoning all peoples to rebellion, destroying anything that bears an Austrian stamp, to come to the aid of the Magyars, the Poles; in a word, to fight against you yourself, Sire!

Moravia—tied to Bohemia from of old by its historical memories, customs, language, and never ceasing to view Prague as its capital and at this time having a special relationship with it through its clubs—Moravia, I thought, is bound to follow the Bohemian movement. The Slovaks and Austrian Silesia will also be carried along with Moravia. In this manner the revolution will embrace a vast region, rich in resources, whose center will be Prague. The revolutionary government with unlimited dictatorial power must sit in Prague. The gentry and all actively opposed clergy will be driven out; the Austrian administration will be ground to dust; all bureaucrats will be driven out, except that some of the senior ones who know more will be kept in Prague for advice and as a library for statistical information. All clubs and journals, all manifestations of garrulous anarchy will also be destroyed, and all will be subjugated to a single dictatorial authority. Youth and all capable people, divided into categories according to the character, abilities, and inclination of each, would be sent throughout the whole region to give it a provisional revolutionary and military organization. The masses of the people would have to be divided into two parts: some, armed, but armed haphazardly, would remain at home to protect the new order, and would be used for partisan warfare if such were to occur. But the young people and all the have-nots capable of bearing arms, factory workers and unemployed artisans, and also the greater part of the educated petty bourgeois youth would constitute the regular troops, not the *Freischaren*,* but troops that would be formed with the aid of former Polish officers and also retired Austrian soldiers and noncommissioned officers, promoted to various officer ranks according to their ability and zeal. The expenses would have been tremendous, but I hoped that they would be covered in part by confiscated estates, and by extraordinary taxes and paper currency similar to Kossuth's. For this I had a special, more or less fantastic financial plan that it is inappropriate to set forth here.

Such was the plan that I devised for a revolution in Bohe-

* Irregulars.

mia. I have set forth its general features without going into further details, for it did not begin to be realized and was known to no one, or was known only in very small, most innocent fragments. And it existed only in my guilty head, and even there it was not formed suddenly but gradually, changing and expanding in accordance with circumstances. And now, not pausing for a political and moral or politically criminal criticism of this plan, I must show you, Sire, what means I had for putting such huge conceptions into effect.

First, I arrived in Leipzig without a kopeck. I did not even have enough for my own meager subsistence, and if Reichel had not quickly sent me a small sum I definitely would not have known how and on what to live, because in good conscience I could ask and demand money from others for my undertakings, but not for myself. I had to have money: "Sans argent point de Suisses," * says the old French proverb, and I had to create absolutely everything: relations with Bohemia, relations with the Magyars; I had to create a party in Prague that would correspond to my wishes, one on which I could later rely for further action. I say "create" because when I arrived in Leipzig there was still not even the shadow of a beginning of any activity; everything existed only in my thoughts. I could not demand money from d'Ester and Hexamer; their means were very limited, despite the fact that the two of them constituted the Central Democratic Committee for the whole of Germany. They collected a sort of tax from all German democrats, but it was insufficient even to cover their own political expenses. I counted on the Poles, but the Poles did not respond to my call. My new relations with them—particularly, with the Polish democrats—began in Dresden, and I can say in good conscience that until March 1849, never in my life had I had political contacts with the Poles, and those into which I was about to enter with them in March did not succeed in developing. And so I had no money, and could I undertake anything without money? I was on the point of going to Paris, partly for money and partly to enter into relations

* "No money, no Swiss," or "Nothing for nothing."

with the French and Polish democracies, and finally also to make the acquaintance there of Count Teleki [110]—the former envoy or, more accurately, agent of Kossuth with the French government—and through him establish relations with Kossuth himself. But thinking it over, I rejected this idea; I rejected it for the following reasons. It was known to me, particularly through my friend Reichel, that as a result of slanderous correspondence in the *Rheinische Zeitung* the French democrats also had doubts about me. When my *Appeal to the Slavs* was printed, I sent one copy to Flocon and included a long letter. In this letter I set forth for him, in accordance with my ideas at that time, the situation in Germany and the status of the Slav question. I informed him of my understanding and complete agreement with the central society of German democrats,* of the second revolution that was being readied in Germany, and of my intentions concerning the Slavs, and Bohemia in particular. I urged him to send to Leipzig, where I was preparing to go, a trusted French democrat who would bring the proposed German-Slav movement into contact with the French movement. Finally, I reproached him for the fact that he could believe the slanderous rumors, and I ended my letter with the solemn announcement that, as the only Russian in the camp of the European democrats, I was bound to guard my honor more strictly than would anyone else, and that if he did not answer me now and prove by positive action that he trusted my honor unconditionally, I would consider myself bound to break off all relations with him. Flocon did not answer me and sent no one, but, probably to show his sympathy for me, reprinted all of my *Appeal* in his journal. The Poles did the same in their journal *Demokrata Polski,* but I read neither the one nor the other in Leipzig, and took Flocon's silence as an insulting lack of faith. [111] Therefore I could not bring myself—even for a goal I considered sacred—to seek a new rapprochement with him or his party, to say nothing of the Polish democrats, who were, if not the first inventors, then doubtless the chief disseminators of my undeserved disgrace. Given such relations

* See n. 137.

with the French and the Poles, I could not promise myself much benefit from an acquaintance with Count Teleki, knowing that he was a close friend of members of the Polish emigration. Thus, thinking better of it, I was convinced that a trip to Paris would be only a vain expenditure of time; and time was precious, for only a few months remained until spring. And so this time, too, I was obliged to give up all hope of contacts and large funds; for all expenses I was obliged to be content with the voluntary assistance of the poor people of Leipzig, and later of the Dresden democrats; and I do not think that in the course of the whole time from January to May 1849 I spent more than 400 thalers, or at the most 500. Such were the funds with which I hoped to raise all Bohemia! And now I shall pass to my contacts and actions.

In my foreign depositions I stated several times that I in no way participated in the activities of the German democrats preparatory to a revolution in Germany in general or in Saxony in particular. And now I must, in good conscience and in accord with the simple truth, repeat the same thing. I wished for a revolution in Germany, wished for it with all my heart. I wished for it as a democrat; I also wished for it because, in my presuppositions, it was to be the sign and, as it were, the point of departure for the Bohemian revolution. But I myself definitely did not contribute in any way to its success, with the possible sole exception of my words of approval and encouragement to all the German democrats I knew. But I did not visit either their clubs or their meetings.[112] I did not ask them about anything; I affected indifference and did not want even to hear of their preparations, although I heard much almost against my will. As for myself, I was occupied exclusively with propaganda in Bohemia. From the Germans I expected and demanded only two things.

First, that they completely change their attitudes and feelings toward the Slavs, that they publicly and loudly proclaim their sympathy for the Slav democrats and recognize Slav independence in positive terms. Such a demonstration seemed necessary to me, necessary in order to bind the Germans themselves with a positive and loudly proclaimed obligation.

It seemed necessary in order to act strongly on the opinion of all the other German democrats and force them to look at the Slav movement through other, more sympathetic eyes. And finally, it seemed necessary in order to overcome the ingrained hatred of the Slavs for the Germans and thus bring them as allies and friends into the society of the European democracies. I must say that d'Ester and Hexamer fully kept their word to me, for in a short time and solely through their efforts almost all German democratic journals, clubs, and congresses suddenly began to speak a quite different language and in most positive terms of the attitudes of Germany toward the Slavs, completely and unconditionally recognizing the right of the latter to independent existence, summoning them to unite with the common European revolutionary cause, offering them alliance and aid against the Frankfurt claims, as well as against all other reactionary German parties. Such a strong, unanimous, and entirely unexpected demonstration also had the desired effect on others: not only the Polish democrats,* but the French democrats, the French democratic journals, and even the Italian democrats in Rome also began to speak of the Slavs as possible and desirable allies. For their part the Slavs, especially the Czech democrats, astonished and gladdened by this sudden change, in turn also began to express in Czech journals their sympathy for European and even German and Magyar democrats. In such a manner was the first step toward rapprochement made.[113]

But this was not all. It was necessary to overcome the hatred of the Bohemian Germans for the Czechs, not only to mollify their hostile feelings but to persuade them to unite with the Czechs in the common revolutionary cause. This was not an easy task, for hatred is always stronger and deeper when it exists between peoples who live near one another and who are in continual contact with each other. Moreover, the hatred between the Germans and the Czechs in Bohemia was a fresh hatred based on burning memories, stirred up and embittered by the unremitting efforts of the Austrian government. This

* Polonskii has "Polish democrats in Paris"; not in Steklov.

hatred was awakened for the first time at the beginning of the revolution of 1848 as a result of two antagonistic, mutually destructive tendencies of both nationalities. The Czechs, who make up two-thirds of the Bohemian population, wanted Bohemia—and quite rightly so, I say—to be an exclusively Slav country, completely independent of Germany. And therefore they did not want to send deputies to the Frankfurt Assembly. The Germans, on the contrary, on the basis of the fact that Bohemia had always belonged to the German Union and had been an integral part of the ancient German Empire since ancient times, demanded its final union, amalgamation with a *newly revived Germany.* The Czechs did not even want to hear of the Viennese ministry; the Germans did not want to recognize any authority other than the Viennese ministers. Thus savage strife ensued, inflamed by Innsbruck on the one hand and on the other by the Viennese government, so that when Prague rebelled in June 1848, the Germans rose from all sides * of German Bohemia and came rushing in crowds of volunteers (*Freischaren*) to the aid of the Austrian troops. General Prince Windischgrätz received them rather coldly, however, and, thanking them, sent them home. From that time enmity between the Czechs and the Germans never ceased and it was not easy to overcome it. Hexamer and d'Ester were very helpful to me in this connection, just as were the Saxon democrats: several times in their own name they sent agents into the German part of Bohemia, on which they acted ceaselessly and indefatigably also through the democrats living along the entire Saxon border, so that by as early as May a large number of Germans in Bohemia were converted to the new faith, and although I did not have direct relations with them, I know that many were ready to unite with the Czechs for the common revolution. My relations with the German democrats were limited to this; in their own matters, I repeat once again, I did not interfere.[114] Now I shall turn to the Czechs.

Only Arnold came to Leipzig in response to my call. I was glad for even this, however, having learned to be satisfied

---

* Polonskii has "from all three sides"; not in Steklov.

with little. All told, he remained in Leipzig only twenty-four hours, despite my efforts to detain him longer. In such a short time I could not question him closely on Bohemia and Prague or fully convey my thoughts to him. Moreover, at least three-fourths of this time was spent in useless conversations with d'Ester and Hexamer. They had gotten the idea of publicly summoning a Slav-German congress in Leipzig—even at that time the Germans had not yet been able to cure themselves completely of their unfortunate passion for congresses—but I resolutely opposed this absurd project. All told, four or at the most five hours were left to me for serious face-to-face talks with Arnold. I tried to use them, to the extent that it was possible, to persuade Arnold to be my accomplice, to act in concert with me, following my course and in my spirit.[115]

On the basis of all the aforementioned reasons, conclusions, and arguments, I attempted to convince him of the necessity of hastening the revolution in Bohemia. And for the attainment of this goal—knowing that he had great influence on the Czech youth, the poor Czech petty bourgeoisie, and especially the Czech peasants, whom he knew well, having long been the manager of the estates of Count Rohan,[116] for whom he was now writing almost exclusively in his democratic, vernacular journal—I asked him to use this influence for revolutionary propaganda. I asked him to organize—first in Prague and then in all Bohemia—a secret society, the plan for which was ready, having been created by me alone. This plan in its main outlines was as follows.

The society was to consist of three separate societies, independent of one another and unknown to one another. They were to have different names: one society was to be for the petty bourgeoisie, a second for youth, and a third for the villages. Each was to be subordinate to a strict hierarchy and to unconditional discipline, but in its details and forms each was to correspond to the character and strength of the class for which it was intended. These societies were to be limited to a small number of people, including—as far as possible—all the talented, learned, energetic, and influential people, who, obeying central directions, would in their turn act invisibly, as it were, on the crowd. All three societies were to be linked by means of a central committee that was to consist of three, at the most five, members: myself and Arnold, and the others would have to be chosen. By means of a secret society I hoped to hasten revolutionary preparations in Bohemia; I hoped that they would be made in all areas according to a single plan. I expected that my secret society, which was not to be disbanded after the revolution, but on the contrary was to grow in strength, expand, enlarging itself with all new vital and really powerful elements, gradually encompassing all the Slav lands—I expected, I say, that it would also provide people for various appointments and positions in the revolutionary hierarchy. Finally, I hoped that through it I would foster and strengthen my influence in Bohemia, for at this same time, without Arnold's knowledge, I had entrusted a young man, a German from Vienna (the student Ottendorfer, who later fled to America),[117] to organize a society among the Bohemian Germans according to this very same plan. I would not have openly participated in its central committee at first, but would have been its secret leader so that, if my project had been realized, all the main threads of the movement would have been concentrated in my hands and I could have been assured that the contemplated revolution in Bohemia did not stray from the course I had prescribed for it. Now concerning the revolutionary government—of how many people it should consist and what form it should take—I had as yet no definite thoughts. I wanted first to become more closely acquainted with the people themselves, as well as with the circumstances; I did not know whether I would participate openly in it, but I had no doubt that I would participate in it, and participate directly and forcefully. Not pride and not ambition but conviction based on a year's experience, conviction that no one among the democrats I knew would be capable of grasping all the conditions of the revolution and of taking those decisive, energetic measures that I considered necessary for its triumph, forced me finally to abandon my former modesty.[118]

Finally, through Arnold and his followers in Prague, I wanted to take control of the Slav Linden, the Czech or, more correctly, the Slav patriotic society recognized as the center of all Slav societies and clubs in the whole Austrian Empire. In general I did not attribute great importance to clubs; I did not like them and even disdained them, seeing in them only gatherings for stupid boasting or empty and even harmful twaddle. But the Slav Linden was an exception to the general rule; it was founded on practical and vital principles by intelligent, practical people. It was the intensified political continuation of the organization and activity of that mighty literary propaganda which, before the revolution of 1848, awakened and, one might say, created a new Slav life. At the same time, it was also the vital center of all the political activities of the Austrian Slavs; and it sent out branches, it had affiliated societies not only in Bohemia but actually in all the Slav lands of the Austrian Empire, with the sole exception of Galicia.[119] It enjoyed such general respect that all Slav leaders considered themselves honored to be members. Even Ban Jelačić himself, advancing on Vienna, felt it necessary to write the society a letter in which, as though excusing his actions, he argued that he was moving against Vienna not because Vienna had carried out a new revolution and was now following a democratic policy, but because it was the center of the German national party.[120] Slav patriots of all parties participated on an equal basis in the Slav Linden. At first the party of Palacký, the Slovak Štúr, and Jelačić predominated; but subsequently—and my brochure *Appeal to the Slavs* may have contributed somewhat to this—the number of democrats in it grew noticeably larger, and one even began to hear shouts of "Élyen Kossuth!" * rather often. And toward the end, the entire Czech Linden definitely deviated from its former course and, loudly proclaiming its sympathy for the Magyars, did not want to send money any more either to the Slovaks or to the South Slavs who were fighting against Kossuth.[121] It was rather easy to take control of the Slav Linden at that time, and in the hands of the Czech democrats it could become a rather powerful and effective means for the attainment of my goals.

Arnold was rather startled and, as it were, disturbed by the

* "Long live Kossuth!"

audacity of these last. He did promise me much, however, but unclearly, timidly, vaguely, complaining now of the lack of money, now of his poor health, so that when he left Leipzig the impression remained with me that I had attained almost nothing by meeting and talking with him. When we were taking leave of one another, however, he promised to write from Prague and to call me when everything was even to some extent prepared for the beginning of further, decisive actions. I had to be satisfied with his vague promises, for at that time I had absolutely no other ways or means for propaganda. When I remember now the meager means with which I planned to accomplish a revolution in Bohemia, it seems laughable to me; I do not understand how I could have hoped for success. But at the time nothing could have stopped me. I reasoned in this manner: A revolution is necessary, hence it is possible. I was not myself; there was a devil of destruction in me. My will, or better, my stubbornness, grew as the difficulties grew, and the numerous obstacles not only did not frighten me, but on the contrary inflamed my revolutionary thirst, inciting me to feverish, untiring activity. I was doomed to destruction; I had a presentiment of this, and I moved gladly toward it. I was then already weary of life.

Arnold did not write to me; once more I knew nothing of Bohemia. Then, taking advantage of the journey to Vienna of a certain young man (Heimberger, the son of an Austrian official, later fled to America) whom I also partially initiated into my secrets, I asked him to stop at Arnold's on his way back and to write to me from Prague.[122] He stayed there for good, of his own free will, and became my regular correspondent. In this way I learned that, although Arnold was apparently doing little and that badly, the disposition of minds in Prague was becoming daily more lively, more resolute, more in keeping with my wishes. I then decided to go to Prague myself and also to persuade the Straka brothers to return to Bohemia. This was in the middle or at the end of March or perhaps even at the beginning of April, new style; I have forgotten all the dates. They have been precisely fixed in the acts of indictment, however.

Now for the first time people began to talk of Russian intervention in the Hungarian war and of the entry of Russian
troops into Hungary to aid the Austrian troops. This news
prompted me to write a second *Appeal to the Slavs* (it was later
printed in the *Dresdner Zeitung* and is found among the acts of
indictment), in which, just as in the first, but with even
greater energy and in more popular language, I summoned the
Slavs to revolution and to war against the Austrians and also
against the Russian troops, although they were Slavic, "so
lange diese den verhängnissvollen Nahmen des Kaisers Nikolai in ihrem Munde führen!" * This appeal was quickly translated into Czech by the Straka brothers and printed in Leipzig
in both languages in a large number of copies. I entrusted the
Czech edition to the Straka brothers and the German edition
to the Saxon democrats for rapid distribution in Bohemia.[123]

I went to Prague by way of Dresden. I stayed in Dresden
several days, became acquainted with several of the chief
leaders of the Saxon democratic party, although without any
definite purpose in mind, not having either letters of recommendation or instructions for them from Leipzig. I became
acquainted with them, I might say, by chance in a democratic
Kneipe,† through Dr. Wittig, with whom I had been acquainted since my first stay in Dresden in 1842.[124] I also became acquainted with, among others, the democratic deputy
Röckel, with whom I later entered into the closest relations
and who subsequently played an active role in the revolutionary attempts in Dresden and Prague.[125] My new, now positive relations with the Poles also began in Dresden. This happened in the following manner.

In Dresden, quite by accident, I met the Galician émigré and
very active member of the democratic society Krzyżanowski.[126] I had first become acquainted with him in Brussels
in 1847, but at that time I had no political relations with
him. Now he was in Dresden on his way to Paris from Galicia,
whence apparently he was forced to flee from persecution by
the Austrian police. We met as old acquaintances, and after

* "As long as the fateful name of Tsar Nicholas is on their lips."
† Tavern.

preliminary greetings I began to reproach him for the slander spread against me by the Polish democrats. To this he replied that neither he nor his friend Heltman, with whom he had lived in Galicia, ever believed empty rumors, that they contradicted them everywhere and always, and that, on the contrary, they wished I would come to Galicia, where I might be useful to them, and were even preparing to write to me but did not know my address.[127] In what and how I might have been useful to them in Galicia, he did not tell me. Thus, after a rather long conversation on general topics, finding in his thoughts much similarity to mine, and noting in him a wish to become close to me, I revealed to him my intentions concerning a Bohemian revolution. Without going into any details, I told him that I had connections in Bohemia and that I was now going to Prague to speed up revolutionary preparations, that I had long wished to unite with the Poles in order to act together with them, but that up to this time all my efforts for a rapprochement with them not only had been without success but had even brought infamous slander upon me. He enthusiastically shared my thoughts concerning the Slavs and asked my permission to discuss this matter officially, one might say, in my name, with the Centralizacja.

I was happy to do this, and he and I agreed on the following points: (1) The Centralizacja would send two trusted representatives who, with me, would make preparations in Dresden for the Bohemian revolution; and who, when the revolution began, would enter with me into a Central All-Slav Committee in which representatives of other Slav peoples would also participate as far as possible. (2) The Centralizacja would undertake the recruitment of Polish officers for the revolution in Bohemia, would send money, and finally would even persuade Count Teleki to send on his part a Magyar agent with sufficient funds to act with us to influence the Magyar regiments then stationed in Bohemia and also for permanent communication with Teleki and Kossuth. (3) We also wanted to establish in Dresden a German-Slav committee to coordinate revolutionary preparations in Bohemia with those in Saxony; but this last project was never even begun, for, as I shall explain later in more detail, there were no special preparations in Saxony. And one may say that all the remaining points, save perhaps the arrival from the Centralizacja of Heltman and Krzyżanowski with empty hands, were also unrealized. All that I obtained this time from my meeting with Krzyżanowski was an English passport, with which I went to Prague, having taken leave of Krzyżanowski, who set out at the same time for Paris.[128]

I was most unpleasantly surprised in Prague, finding nothing ready there, absolutely nothing. The secret society had not even been started, and no one, it seemed, was even thinking of an imminent revolution. I started to reproach Arnold, but he laid all the blame on his poor health. Later, it seems, he was much more active; I say "it seems" because to the very end I thought he was doing nothing, and only from the Austrian commission of inquiry did I learn, if this is true, that he later acted zealously and forcefully, but at the same time so cautiously that even the people who were closest to him did not suspect his activity. Besides Arnold, one evening I had a meeting with a large number of Czech democrats who came to my place by invitation, but came—to my great displeasure—in numbers surpassing my expectations. The meeting was noisy, confused, and left me with the impression that the Prague democrats were great talkers and that they were more inclined to facile and vain rhetoric than to dangerous undertakings. Now it seems that I frightened them with the sharpness of several of the expressions that burst from me. It seemed to me that none of them understood the sole conditions under which a Bohemian revolution was possible. Just like the Germans— from whom, by the way, the Czechs had in general learned much, despite all their hatred for them—all of them were more or less infected with a passion for clubs and a faith in the efficaciousness of empty chatter. I also became convinced that if I left them enough room for their pride and yielded them all the trappings of power, it would not be difficult for me to seize real power when the revolution began. I subsequently saw several of them in private and, noticing that several other undertakings—less decisive, with more remote prospects, but nevertheless inclining to one and the same revolutionary goal—paralleled my plans, I began to think of means of using them.[129] For this purpose I should have stayed in Prague, but this was definitely impossible; for despite all my efforts to keep my presence secret, the Prague democrats were so garrulous that the following day not only the whole democratic party but all the Czech liberals knew I was in Prague, and since the Austrian government even then was pursuing me because of my first *Appeal to the Slavs*, without a doubt I would have been arrested had I not left in time.[130]

For lack of other resources, I was obliged to place all my hopes on the Straka brothers, whose minds I had been able to cultivate and nourish with my spirit, so to speak, through seeing them daily and hourly for more than two months. I gave them full and detailed instructions concerning all preparations for revolution in Prague and in Bohemia in general. I authorized them to act for me and in my name, and although I do not know well or in detail what they subsequently did, I must declare myself responsible for their slightest actions, responsible and a thousand times more guilty than they.

My short stay in Prague was enough to convince me that I was not mistaken in hoping to find in Bohemia all necessary elements for a successful revolution. Bohemia was then really in complete anarchy. The new gains of the March revolution (*die Märzerrungenschaften,** a favorite expression at that time), already suppressed in other parts of the Austrian Empire, were still in full bloom in Bohemia. The Austrian government still had need of the Slavs and therefore did not wish, even feared, to touch them with reactionary measures. Because of this, in Prague as well as in all Bohemia, unlimited freedom of clubs, popular meetings, and book publishing still reigned; this freedom extended so far that Viennese students and other Viennese refugees, who at that time were being shot in Vienna, walked the streets of Prague openly under their own names, without the slightest danger. All the people in the cities as well as in the villages were armed and everywhere dis-

* The March gains.

satisfied: dissatisfied and distrustful because they felt the approach of reaction and feared the loss of their newly acquired rights. In the villages they feared the threatening aristocracy and the restoration of their former subjection. Finally, dissatisfied to the highest degree because of the newly raised levy of recruits, they were really everywhere ready for rebellion. Moreover, there were then very few troops in Bohemia, and those consisted mostly of Magyar regiments that felt an insuperable inclination to mutiny. When students met Magyar soldiers on the street and greeted them with the shout "Élyen Kossuth!" the soldiers would answer them with the same shout, paying no attention to their officers who were present and listening. When Magyar soldiers were sent to arrest a student for swearing or for scuffling with the police, the soldiers would join the students and together they would give the police officers a beating. In a word, the disposition of the Magyar regiments was such that no sooner had the revolutionary movement begun in Dresden than the half-squadron stationed on the border, hearing of it, revolted and came galloping into Saxony without being called at all. More than two years have passed since then, and during the course of this time the Austrian government has doubtless used all possible means to root out the revolutionary Kossuth spirit of the Magyar troops. But this spirit had put down such deep roots in the heart of every Magyar—even more among the simple than among the educated—that I am convinced that if a war should start even now, the cry "Élyen Kossuth!" would be enough to cause them to rebel and go over to the side of the enemy. And at that time there was no doubt of it; I was firmly convinced that on the first day, at the first hour, they would unite with the Bohemian revolution—an important gain, for in this way a strong beginning for a revolutionary army in Bohemia would be made. Finally, to fill out the picture, one must also add that Austrian finances were in a most pitiful condition at that time. In Bohemia not state but private paper money was in circulation; every banker, every merchant had his own notes; there were even wooden and leather coins, such as those that exist among peoples who are at the lowest stage of civilization.

There were therefore many revolutionary elements. It was necessary only to gain control of them, but I definitely lacked the means to do this. I still did not despair, however. I commissioned the Straka brothers to set up secret societies hastily in Prague, not holding strictly to the old plan, which there was no longer enough time to carry out, but concentrating their main attention on Prague in order to prepare the city as soon as possible for the revolutionary movement. I particularly asked them to open communications with the workers and to form gradually from among the most reliable people a force of 500, 400, or 300 people (depending upon possibilities), a kind of revolutionary battalion on which I could rely unconditionally and with whose aid I could gain control of all the other less organized or completely unorganized Prague elements. Having gained control of Prague, I hoped to gain control of all Bohemia as well; for I intended to compel the main leaders of the Czech democracy to unite with me, to compel them either by conviction or by satisfying their pride, presenting them as aforesaid with all honors and emoluments of power, but if neither one was effective, then by force. Finally I asked them to seek acquaintance with everyone, but not to express an opinion, not to babble, to be unpretentious, not to insult anyone's vanity, but to observe carefully all movements and all parallel undertakings, in the apprehension that they might anticipate us. And I asked them to write to me in Dresden, giving everything in all possible detail, and I promised to send them money and, when the time came, to come myself with the Polish officers.

Soon after my return to Dresden, Krzyzanowski and Heltman arrived on behalf of the democratic Centralizacja.* They brought me nothing, not money, not Polish officers, not a Magyar agent, but only heartfelt sympathy and a multitude of compliments from the Polish as well as the Paris democrats.

* They arrived in Dresden about the middle of April (possibly 13 April) 1849, according to Steklov.

Concerning the money, I learned that the Centralizacja itself was incredibly poor, just as were the French democrats, who were exhausted by the June Days of the previous year. I learned that there would be Polish officers, and they would be in large numbers, from France as well as from the Duchy of Poznań, just as soon as the money necessary to bring them was found. And finally I learned that Count Teleki was rich in means but that he had not made up his mind to enter into relations with us or to make Magyar money available for the Bohemian movement, not having received permission to do so from Kossuth, to whom he had written concerning this matter and from whom he was awaiting an answer. Thus I was in no condition to keep a single one of the promises that I had given first to the Straka brothers, and later, through them, to Arnold and other Czech democrats who had entered into relations with them after my departure from Prague. I was obliged to support the Straka brothers in Prague, and for this, like a beggar, I had to ask for charity from all my acquaintances and did not receive a kopeck from a single one except the afore-mentioned deputy Röckel, a careless, garrulous, eccentric, but zealous democrat who even sold his furniture to supply me with at least some funds.

I subsequently became acquainted with the now deceased Baron Baier, formerly an officer in the Austrian service and who had later taken part in the Hungarian uprising.[131] For a time he commanded a Magyar detachment, I do not remember in what Hungarian fortress. He was severely wounded and as a consequence, having left Hungary, became—I do not know how—an agent of Count Teleki in Dresden, where it seems he was engaged exclusively in the recruitment of officers for the Magyar army. He showed me a letter from Count Teleki in which the latter questioned him about Bohemia. I used this opportunity to persuade him to write a letter to Teleki at my dictation, informing him on my behalf of the imminent Bohemian revolution, presenting to him all the advantageous results that were bound to follow from it for the Magyars themselves, and demanding finally that he send a representative with money. Teleki replied that he would come himself; and apparently he really was in Dresden, but too late, for I was then already in prison. This was the extent of my relations with the Magyars.

Meanwhile my correspondence with the Straka brothers continued.[132] They demanded money. I sent them as much as I could; i.e., very little. But I consoled them with future hopes; I urged them to stand firm just as I myself was standing firm at that time, and, not looking back, not stopping, disregarding all difficulties and obstacles, to prepare the revolution and to call me when the hour for the uprising drew near. They were in reality very active, as I subsequently learned from the commission of inquiry. I could not learn much from their letters, they were so vague and obscure. I have now told everything concerning my Bohemian undertakings and activities, of which sending Röckel to Prague was the last.[133]

But first * I shall tell the nature of my reactions to the newly arrived Poles, namely, to Heltman and Krzyżanowski. I can say with complete justice that there were definitely none. Between us even at that time there was not complete confidence, neither on their part nor on mine: they never said even half a word to me about their Polish affairs, with which they were much more concerned, it seemed to me, than with Bohemian matters. This was, by the way, not difficult, for they were not at all concerned with the latter. Repaying reticence with reticence, I for my part also secretly held back much from them. I showed them only the superficial aspects of my own plans and did not permit them to enter into direct relations with Bohemia. I alone corresponded with Prague, and all that they knew they knew solely through me. When I received bad news I held it back; but when the news was good I tried to exaggerate it for their eyes. In a word, I kept them at some distance from all actual conditions and preparations and considered myself justified in acting in this manner toward them, for I saw clearly that the Centralizacja, which had not sent me any assis-

---

* I.e., Steklov notes, before the description of Saxon affairs.

tance with them, not money or officers or a Magyar agent, had sent me only these two, not really to make common cause with me but to take control of the Bohemian movement as much as possible and use it to gain their own ends (unknown to me), in accord with their exclusively Polish orientation. I saw Heltman and Krzyzanowski often, almost every day, but more as a friend than as an accomplice. We seldom spoke of the Bohemian preparations; they seldom even asked me about them, either because they noticed my lack of frankness or perhaps also because, having ceased to expect great results from the preparations, they were more interested in other matters unknown to me. In only one matter did we reach positive agreement, namely, on the necessity of establishing in Prague an all-Slav revolutionary committee when the revolution began. We left everything else to future inspiration and circumstances. They probably had their own plans, and I, counting on my superior influence in Prague, firmly intended to remove them just as soon as they proved to be adversaries. Heltman and Krzyżanowski also had connections in Dresden completely independent of mine. But to finish my story I shall now turn to the Germans for the last time.

The Germans are definitely a strange people, and judging by what I saw when I lived among them I do not think that fate has a long political existence in store for them. When I said that the German democrats had lately started to become centralized, I meant that they had finally comprehended the necessity of centralized activity and centralized authority. They spoke much and often of this, and even made some moves as though they were centralized, but there was no real centralization among them, despite the existence of the Central Democratic Committee. Having chosen this committee, they thought they had done everything and did not consider it necessary to subordinate themselves to it. What makes the French democrats dangerous and powerful is their extraordinary spirit of discipline: Frenchmen of differing characters, classes, and positions, of differing tendencies, even of different parties, are able to unite to achieve a common goal, and once they are united, then neither pride nor ambition, absolutely nothing is

capable of dividing them until the proposed goal is attained.*
Among the Germans, ON THE OTHER HAND, ANARCHY PRE-
DOMINATES. THE FRUIT OF PROTESTANTISM AND OF THE WHOLE
POLITICAL HISTORY of Germany, anarchy is the basic feature of
the German mind, of the German character, and of German
life: anarchy between the provinces, anarchy between the cities and villages; anarchy among the inhabitants of one and the
same locality, among the frequenters of one and the same circle; finally, IN EVERY GERMAN TAKEN INDIVIDUALLY, ANARCHY
AMONG HIS MIND, HIS HEART, AND HIS WILL. "JEDER DARF UND
SOLL SEINE MEINUNG HABEN!" † This is the first confession of
the German catechism, a rule by which every German, without exception, is guided. And for this reason, no political
unity among them has been or will be possible.

So, at this very time, when the closest unity of all democrats
and all liberals was necessary in order to struggle with some
success against triumphant reaction, not only the democrats
and the liberals and not only the democrats of all Germany,‡
but even the democrats of one and the same German state
could not, did not know how, and even did not wish to unite.
"Jeder wollte seine Meinung haben." § All were disunited by
petty rivalry, more vain than ambitious. Thus, neither Breslau
nor Cologne wanted to submit to Berlin, and at the same time
even fought each other. Königsberg was all by itself, Prussian
Saxony too. I am not speaking of Brandenburg and Pomerania,
which constantly stood on the side of the monarchy. Even less
am I speaking of the Duchy of Poznań, where at that time
there prevailed the deepest hatred indiscriminately for anything with a German name. Westphalia leaned more toward
Cologne. Hanover, together with the other maritime lands,
constituted a special group that came into contact with the rest
of Germany only through the Schleswig-Holstein war, in

---

* Nicholas' marginal note: "A striking truth!!!" According to Polonskii, Nicholas' marginal note appears opposite the following sentence on anarchy and
the Germans.

† "Each may and ought to have his own opinion." Nicholas' marginal note:
"An irrefutable truth!!!"

‡ Nicholas' marginal note: "True."

§ "Each wished to have his own opinion." Nicholas' marginal note: "True."

which, however, the liberals took a much greater part than the democrats. The democrats of the Kingdom of Saxony had their own central committee, which was also the committee of the Thuringian democrats. Bavaria, excluding the Palatinate and the northern part of Franconia, was scarcely touched by democratic propaganda. The rest of southern Germany—Baden, Württemberg, as well as both the Hesses and the other small duchies—outwardly recognized the Central Committee, for they participated in its selection at the democratic congress in Berlin, but in essence had no regard for it whatsoever, never obeyed its orders, did not even send it money, but grouped themselves mostly around the democrats of the Frankfurt Constituent Assembly, who from the very first competed and quarreled with the northern democrats. So in reality there was no centralization, and the Central Committee of German Democrats was in a most grievous situation.

It was poor, it was not powerful, and finally it consisted of members incapable of the task. Three were chosen to it: d'Ester, Hexamer, and Count Reichenbach; [134] but the last left it at the very start; only Hexamer and d'Ester were active. Hexamer is a young, honorable, innocent, not stupid, but very limited man, slow to understand, a democratic doctrinaire and utopian. D'Ester—I shall not hide from you, Sire, that I am speaking of them in such detail only because I know that they both were saved by flight—d'Ester, on the other hand, is a lively, talented, fast-working man, quickly but superficially understanding, something of a rogue and a sly fox, but not a self-interested political intrigant. He belongs to the school of Cologne democrats (i.e., more or less communistic); he is quick-witted, resourceful, evasive, knows how to bait a minister in a parliamentary debate; in a word, he is gifted in partisan political warfare. He could be a German Duvergier de Hauranne [135] under a German democratic Thiers, if such were to be found in Germany, but he does not have a broad enough mind or enough character to be the leader of a party.

I constantly guarded myself against interference in their affairs. Living in the same house with them for two months or a little less, however, I knew much and can say with certainty and in good conscience that the Central Committee bustled about a great deal but did absolutely nothing for the success of the proposed revolution, despite the fact that it placed its final hopes on the revolution; for d'Ester himself said to me that this would be the decisive and final attempt, and if it did not succeed it would be necessary to postpone all revolutionary plans for a long, long time. And just what were they doing? Instead of putting aside all other matters and concerning themselves exclusively with preparations for the revolution, they spent most of their time on lesser, insignificant matters, on problems that even led them into countless conflicts with numerous sections of the democratic party. They laughed at the Saxons, who firmly believed in the stability of their newly created democratic constitution; they told the Saxons that a second revolution was necessary even to preserve those as yet undestroyed political rights—remnants of the revolutionary gains of 1848—which the reaction had not yet dared touch. They said that without a second revolution everything would be uncertain, shaky; yet they themselves acted as though they had not the slightest doubt of the political foundation on which they stood. D'Ester was much more concerned with his election to the second Prussian Legislative Assembly than with revolutionary preparations; Hexamer busied himself with idle, useless, pompously congratulatory public correspondence with the French, Italian, and Polish democrats. Both of them pleaded for the establishment of a new democratic journal in Berlin, whose editor they wanted to be; they collected subscriptions everywhere and quarreled on this occasion with all the democrats when it was clear that, if there were no second revolution, then the existence of this journal in Berlin would be impossible, and, should the revolution succeed, then all former rushing about, quarrels, and subscriptions would have been utterly in vain. When Arnold arrived in Leipzig, instead of concerning themselves with the sole purpose of his coming—i.e., the uniting of the Bohemian and German movements—or at least questioning him about Bohemia, about which they both knew almost nothing, they spoke with him of almost nothing but their unfortunate journal and the afore-

mentioned Slav-German congress. There were no other conversations, conditions, or agreed-upon measures: "We are
preparing a revolution for the spring; you too try to be ready
by that time"—that is all that Arnold heard from them. From
this alone one can see the nature of their preparations and
measures for revolution in Germany itself.

I do not say that they did absolutely nothing and did not
think at all of preparations for revolution; I say only that their
actions were insignificant, insufficient, and did not contribute
in the slightest to the success of the revolution. I know, for instance, that they organized secret societies in various places in
Germany, but these societies had no influence in the May all-
German uprising. Neither do I doubt but that they had contacts with several of the main leaders in the democratic party
in various parts of Germany, although I do not have any positive information on this either. But I definitely know that they
quarreled with many people: with Breslau, with the central
committee of Saxon democrats, and finally even in Frankfurt
they had many more enemies than friends, so that on the eve
of the Baden revolution the south German democrats not only
opposed their interference but even asked them not to
come.[136] I learned of this situation from a peculiar incident
about which I shall speak later.

I might be asked: If the Central Committee was really so
powerless and inactive, how could it have produced in all of
Germany the aforementioned unanimous and powerful demonstration in favor of the Slavs, and where did it suddenly
acquire the energy and drive and influence for such indefati-
gable propaganda among the Bohemian Germans? To this I
shall answer the following: Nothing was easier than to produce such a demonstration; they had both sufficient influence
and all necessary means for it; they were in correspondence
with all the democratic journals and, moreover, had the addresses of all the main leaders of committees and clubs, whom
they often influenced, bypassing the commitees, through influential people they knew. Of course there is nothing easier
than persuading any German in any matter as long as he
thinks himself independent and does not suspect that you

want to subject him to some discipline or other. I composed articles that d'Ester and Hexamer sent to journals in their own names. I had them write in my presence, almost at my dictation, a common letter to all the clubs, and gave them no rest until they had done everything that seemed necessary to me. Thus in many journals there suddenly appeared articles sympathetic to the Slavs; and the clubs, already prepared by letters and explanations from the Central Committee, followed their example and began to compose high-flown addresses to the Slavs. Once begun, this movement then continued without any outside pressure. Propaganda in Bohemia would also not have been carried out if I had not continually pressed the members of the Central Committee and, even more, the Leipzig democrats I knew, who in turn acted through their friends living on the Bohemian border. And all this was done without special measures, conspiracies, agreements, but simply through good friendship.

Once more I repeat, there was much general talk throughout all Germany of the imminent revolution, but there was definitely no common conspiracy, no common organization, no plan for central direction and action, despite the fact that a central committee for central direction and central action was chosen. The universality of the German uprising in May 1849 was much more the fruit of the unanimous action of the German governments than of agreement among the German democrats. Everyone had known for half a year that there would be a revolution in the spring because they had finally come to understand that the governments, having once successfully started a reactionary movement, would not stop halfway and would not rest until the old order, destroyed by the revolution of 1848, was completely restored. Everyone expected even more drastic reactionary measures by spring, and everyone was preparing to answer them with a revolutionary rebuff and was waiting for the inevitable collision—foreseen by everyone—of the Frankfurt parliament with the rulers of Germany as a signal to everyone for a general uprising. Aside from this there was no unanimity among the German democrats. The actions of the Central Committee were limited to encouraging everyone to prepare for revolution, but it could not and did not know how to become a center for these same preparations. All parts of Germany were preparing by themselves, in their own way, each according to its character, circumstances, situation, independently of the Central Committee and without any contact with one another. And I say once more that the universality of the preparations consisted only in the fact that everyone knew that everyone was preparing; not only the democrats knew, but the opposition party also, because everyone was preparing and even noisily organizing secret societies.

Everyone was preparing, but no one prepared enough. I cannot judge of the activities of the southern democrats, however, because—except for one time that I shall mention later—I did not come into contact with them after the spring of 1848. Apparently something like a real organization existed in Baden. But I can judge of the preparations in Saxony because I saw them near at hand, although I did not participate in them in any way. I know that the Saxons did not have a plan or an organization or even leaders appointed for the insurrection. Everything was left to chance. This was clearly shown in the Dresden revolutionary attempt, which was so little foreseen by the leaders of the democratic party themselves that they were all about to disperse the evening before. And no one—either in Dresden or in the other cities of Saxony—knew that the revolution, long prophesied by all, was beginning precisely now. And when it began, no one knew what to do or where to go; everyone followed his own instinct because nothing was foreseen. It is hard to believe, but in fact that is how it was. I am now trying to gather all my recollections in order to say something positive about the preparations of the Saxon democrats, but I find absolutely nothing unless it is that in several corners of the Saxon land there existed microscopic, trifling secret societies consisting of five, six, at the most ten people, for the most part workers; or that in several cities—namely, in Dresden, in Chemnitz, and then in Leipzig too—some tin hand grenades were manufactured—harmless children's toys, on which, however, the Saxon democrats placed great hopes.

There was no need to prepare weapons and ammunition, however, because all Saxony, like all Germany, had been armed during the previous revolution; and what it was necessary to prepare was a plan for the insurrection, a plan for all Saxony as well as for each city individually; it was necessary to choose people as leaders, to establish a revolutionary hierarchy, to agree upon the first steps, the first measures of the planned revolution; it was necessary to carry revolutionary propaganda from the city to the countryside, to persuade the peasants to take part in the movement so that the revolution would be national, powerful, and not solely urban, not easily defeated. There was not even the beginning of anything like this; all preparations were limited to nonsense. In a word, the Saxon democrats did enough to be later convicted as state criminals, but they did not do enough for the success of the revolution. One could say the same of me also, but with this difference: I was one and they were many. They had all the means and I had none. The Saxon Commission of Inquiry long searched for traces of a conspiracy, of a plan, of preparations for a rebellion, of secret connections between the Saxon democrats and other German democrats, but, finding nothing, in the end consoled itself with the thought that a conspiracy really did in fact exist, a terrible conspiracy with widespread connections, with a deep plan, and with countless means, but that the fugitive Jäkel, the most insignificant of the three very ungifted members of the Saxon Democratic Committee, had carried all its secrets and threads off to London.[137] I say "consoled itself" with this thought because it must have been embarrassing to the German governments that they could have trembled so long before the German democrats. Since everything on earth is relative, however, the German democrats might have been terrifying to the German governments.

But it is time for me to end these general considerations on the pitiful revolutionary activity of the German democrats and, returning to myself, bring my no less pitiful story to a conclusion. Little remains now for me to add.

I have shown in what way my relations with d'Ester and Hexamer, as well as with the Leipzig democrats, were limited.

I have explained why I confidently expected and why I desired a German revolution. I added, in keeping with the truth, that I myself did not interfere in German matters in the slightest. I must also say the same of my stay in Dresden until the very day of the election of the Provisional Government. I was living in Dresden, not for the sake of Saxony or Germany, but solely for the sake of Bohemia; I chose it as my place of residence as it was the closest place to Prague. Just as formerly in Leipzig, here too I did not visit clubs or democratic meetings; on the contrary, I was in hiding, not knowing for certain whether or not the Dresden police would tolerate my presence in Dresden without a passport. I saw few people; I knew many democrats, but I seldom met them. The democrat and deputy Tzschirner— who, I was convinced, was the chief if not the only, although very pitiful, preparer of the Saxon revolution—I saw twice, at the most three times, and not at his place or in my apartment, but in an ordinary democratic tavern.[138] I was very superficially acquainted with him and conversed with him little. The only two Germans with whom I had positive, businesslike relations in Dresden were Dr. Wittig, the editor of a Dresden democratic newspaper,* and the aforementioned democratic deputy August Röckel.[139] The former was useful to me in many ways; the editorial office of his paper served me in place of an office in my Prague dealings. And the paper itself was under my exclusive influence in everything that concerned the Slav question. I was even more closely connected with the democrat Röckel; he greatly facilitated propaganda in German Bohemia through his connections with Saxon democrats along the border. He looked for money for me when money became necessary to me, and, as I have already noted above, he even sold his furniture to make it possible for me to support the Straka brothers; i.e., my only hope for revolution in Prague. I did not hide my undertakings from him, just as he hid nothing from me; but I did not interfere in his German affairs and connections, although, when it was necessary, I made use of the latter for my own ends. Among the German democrats

* *Dresdner Zeitung.*

with whom I was well acquainted—although I had no positive, businesslike relations with them—was a certain Dr.
Erbe.[140] He was an Altenburg democrat, deputy, and exile
who was later chosen—I do not remember by what Saxon
city—for the Frankfurt Paliament. I mention him because my
acquaintance with him brought about my only fortuitous contact with the Baden democrats, whom I mentioned above. It
seems that Erbe, arriving in Frankfurt, took an active part in
the south German movement, and I have been told that he
subsequently betook himself to America. Several days before
the Dresden insurrection, a friend of Erbe's—also a Frankfurt
deputy *—had apparently come to Dresden on other matters
unknown to me. He asked me on behalf of Erbe, and also on
behalf of all the Baden democrats who appealed to me through
him, for a letter of recommendation to the Polish Centralizacja
in Paris; they were in need of Polish officers. I brought him
and Heltman and Krzyżanowski together and thus was the
indirect cause of the appearance of General Sznajde and other
Poles in the Duchy of Baden.[141] Here I saw how strong was the
disagreement between the northern and southern democrats
and how insignificant was the influence of the Central Democratic Committee on the latter. D'Ester, who arrived in Dresden that very same day, met Erbe's Frankfurt friend at my
place. They conversed for a long time about the imminent
Baden and, in general, the south German movement, and
d'Ester said he wished that all democratic members of the forcibly dissolved German parliaments would gather in Frankfurt
to constitute, with the Frankfurt democrats, a new democratic
German parliament. To this Erbe's friend replied that the
Frankfurt democrats, and in general the south German democrats, would ask Messieurs the northern democrats not to interfere in their affairs and not to come to them, but to stay at
home and concern themselves with hastening the revolution
in the north. From this an argument developed, then a quarrel, which it would be out of place to recount here.

With the approach of May, portents of revolution became

* Schlütter, according to Steklov.

clearer from day to day and more fraught with meaning throughout all Germany. The Frankfurt Parliament, which near the end of its existence leaned toward the democrats, was already in obvious collision with the governments. The German constitution was finally concocted; some governments—as, for example, Württemberg—recognized it, but they recognized it against their will, frightened as they were by the manifest threat of a rebellion. The Prussian King rejected the crown offered him; the Saxon government was wavering. [142] Many hoped that it would bow to necessity and that the matter would be handled quietly. Others foresaw a collision. I was among the latter, and, convinced of the imminence of a general German revolution, I encouraged the Straka brothers by letters to strengthen their activity, speed preparations, and proceed to final, decisive measures. But I could not send them money or any other aid except advice and encouragement; I did send them a few thalers, depriving myself of my last means, since at that time I was not spending more than five or six silver groschen a day on myself. There was no money, there were no Polish officers, there was not even the possibility of stirring. Every day I expected Count Teleki. I also expected to be called to Prague soon. I did not know what to do or where to turn; in a word, I was in a most difficult situation.

Finally the Saxon democratic parliament was dissolved. [143] This was the first step toward reaction in Saxony, so that even those who had formerly doubted now began to think of the possibility of a Saxon revolution, which seemed still so distant to everyone, however, that Röckel, fearing persecution, decided to leave Dresden for a time. I persuaded him to go to Prague. I gave him a note to Arnold and Sabina, and also to the Straka brothers, and commissioned him to accelerate preparations for the Prague uprising as much as he could. With whom and how he acted there, and in general what was done in Prague after his departure from Dresden, were unknown to me to the very end, and only from the Austrian commission did I subsequently learn of some of the circumstances. [144] On the day of his departure, and while he was still at my place, Dr. Zimmer came to me, persuaded to do so by my friend and associate Ottendorfer.[145] Dr. Zimmer was a former member of the dissolved Austrian parliament, a zealous democrat, one of the most influential leaders of the German party in Bohemia, and also, before this, one of the most inveterate enemies of the Czech people. After a lengthy and heated argument I succeeded in bringing him over to my side. He bade me farewell, promising to go to Prague immediately and assist in uniting the Germans and Czechs for the revolution. All these circumstances, disclosed not by me but by Dr. Zimmer himself, are set forth in detail in the Austrian acts of indictment. The dispatch of Röckel and Dr. Zimmer were my last acts having to do with Bohemia.

I have told everything, Sire, and, no matter how hard I think, I cannot find a single circumstance of even slight importance that I have omitted here. Now all that remains for me is to explain to you how, having remained until this time a stranger to all German matters, and every day expecting to be called to Prague, I could take part—and such an active part, at that—in the Dresden insurrection.

On the very day after Röckel's departure—i.e., after the dissolution of parliament—disorders began in Dresden. They continued for several days, not yet assuming a decisive character, but they were of such a nature that they could not end otherwise than with revolution or complete reaction.[146] Revolution I did not fear, but I did fear reaction, which would unavoidably end in the arrest of all political refugees without passports and of revolutionary volunteers, among whom I was not the least. For a long time I did not know what to do, for a long time I could not make up my mind to do anything; it seemed dangerous to remain, but it was shameful, definitely impossible, to flee. I was the chief and sole instigator of the Prague conspiracy, both German and Czech; I had sent the Straka brothers to Prague, I had exposed many people to obvious danger there, and thus I did not have the right to flee from danger myself. There was still one thing I could do: withdraw to a place in the vicinity and wait, near Dresden, for the movement to take on a more decisive, revolutionary character. But for this, money was needed, and I do not think I had more than two thalers in my pocket. And Dresden was the center of my correspondence; I was awaiting Count Teleki and at any minute I might be called to Prague. I decided to stay, and persuaded Krzyżanowski and Heltman, who were already quite prepared to leave, to do the same. Having remained, neither by my situation nor by my character could I be an indifferent and passive spectator of the Dresden events. I did, however, refrain from all participation until the very day of the election of the Provisional Government. [147]

I shall not enter into the details of the Dresden insurrection; it is known to you, Sire, and doubtless better known to you in all its scope than it is to me. Moreover, all circumstances concerning me are set forth in detail in the acts of the Saxon Commission of Inquiry. In my opinion, the movement was from the beginning carried out by peaceful citizens, burghers who saw it at first as one of those *innocent* and *legal* gala demonstrations that even at that time had become so much a part of the German way that they neither frightened nor surprised anyone. And when they noticed that the movement was becoming a revolution, they backed off and yielded their place to the democrats, saying that when they swore "mit Gut und Blut für die neu errungene Freiheit zu stehen!" * they had in mind a peaceful, bloodless, and safe protest, and not a revolution. At first the revolution was constitutional, but then it became democratic. Elected to the Provisional Government were two representatives of the monarchical-constitutional party, Heubner and Todt [148] (several days before this, the latter had been the government commissioner who dissolved parliament in the name of the King), and only one democrat, Tzschirner. I had known Todt since my very first stay in Dresden and later saw him in passing in Frankfurt in the spring of 1848. In Dresden I did not meet him again until the day he was elected to the Provisional Government. I did not know Deputy Heubner at all, and I have already stated above the limits of my relations, my acquaintance, with Tzschirner.

When the Provisional Government met, I began to hope for

---

* "To defend the newly won freedom with property and blood!"

the success of the revolution. And indeed, the circumstances on that day were most favorable: there were many people but few troops. The greater part of the Saxon army, which all told was not very numerous, was then fighting for German liberty and unity in Schleswig-Holstein, *stammverwandt und meerumschlungen;* * in Dresden there were, I think, no more than two or three battalions. The Prussian troops had not yet succeeded in coming to their assistance, and nothing would have been easier than to seize all Dresden. Having seized it, and relying on Saxony, which had risen—and risen quite unanimously, although without any method or plan—and relying also on the movement in the rest of Germany, they could also have opposed the Prussian troops, who, just like the Saxons, did not demonstrate great courage in Dresden. They took all of five days for a task that could have been completed in one day, and perhaps less, by more resolute troops; for although there were many armed democrats in Dresden, they were all paralyzed by the disordered revolutionary leadership.

On the day of the election of the Provisional Government my activity was limited to advice. It seems to me it was 4 May, according to the new style. The Saxon troops were parleying; I advised Tzschirner not to let himself be deceived, for it was clear that the government only wanted to gain time while it waited for Prussian aid. I advised Tzschirner to break off idle negotiations, not to lose time, to take advantage of the weakness of the troops in order to seize all Dresden. I also proposed that he even gather the Poles I knew, of whom there were many then in Dresden, and with them lead the people, who were demanding arms, to the armory. The whole day was lost in negotiations; on the next day Tzschirner recalled my advice and my proposal, but conditions had already changed; the burghers had dispersed to their homes with their guns and the people had cooled down. The *Freischaren* † who had arrived were still few in number, but it seems the first Prussian battalions had already appeared. Acceding to his request, however, and even more to his promises, I found Heltman and

* Of one blood and embraced by the sea.
† Irregulars.

Krzyżanowski and not without difficulty persuaded them to participate with me in the Dresden revolution, pointing out to them the favorable results that might come from its successful course, results favorable for the Bohemian revolution that we anticipated. They agreed and brought to the town hall, where the Provisional Government was meeting, yet another Polish officer, whom I, however, did not know.* We then concluded a sort of contract with Tzschirner: he declared to us, first, that if the revolution were successful he would not be satisfied with only the recognition of the Frankfurt Parliament and the Frankfurt constitution, but would proclaim a democratic republic; second, he pledged himself to help us and be our true ally in all our Slav undertakings; he promised us money and arms—in a word, everything that would be needed for the Bohemian revolution. He asked only that we say nothing to Todt and Heubner, whom he called traitors and reactionaries.

So we (Heltman, Krzyżanowski, the above-mentioned Polish officer, and I) settled in a room of the Provisional Government behind screens.[149] Our situation was extremely strange: we constituted a sort of staff alongside the Provisional Government, which carried out all our demands unquestioningly. But Lieutenant Heinze, who held the position of commander of the national guard and commanded the revolutionary militia, acted independently of us and independently even of the Provisional Government itself. He viewed us with obvious hostility, almost with hatred, and not only did not carry out a single one of our demands, transmitted to him in the form of orders of the Provisional Government, but acted at cross-purposes with us, so that all our efforts were in vain. For twenty-four hours we demanded only five hundred or even three hundred, whom we wished to bring to the armory, but we could not collect even fifty, not because there were no men but because Heinze permitted no one to come to us; instead, just as soon as fresh forces arrived, he scattered them all throughout the whole of Dresden. I was then certain and am now convinced that Heinze acted as a traitor, and I do not understand how he

* Steklov identifies him as Władysław Gołębiowski from Galicia.

could be condemned as a state criminal. He contributed much more to the victory of the troops themselves, who, as I have already said, acted very, very timidly. [150]

On the next day (it seems it was the sixth of May) my Poles disappeared, and Tzschirner with them. [151] It happened in this way.

Heubner—I cannot think of this man without special sorrow! I had not known him formerly, but I came to know him during these few days; in such circumstances people quickly come to know each other. I have seldom known a purer, nobler, more honorable man; neither by nature nor by inclination nor by his ideas was he called to revolutionary activity; he was of a peaceful, modest nature; he had just married and was passionately in love with his wife, and felt much more inclined to write sentimental verses for her than to hold a position in the revolutionary government, into which he, just like Todt, had fallen like a chicken into the cabbage soup. It was the fault of his constitutional friends that he found himself in the government; they, taking advantage of his selflessness and hoping to paralyze Tzschirner's democratic plans, had chosen him. And he saw in this revolution a legal, sacred war for German unity, of which he was a fiery and somewhat dreamy worshiper; he thought he did not have the right to refuse a dangerous post, and he agreed. Once having agreed, he wanted to carry out his role honorably to the end; and indeed, he made the greatest sacrifice to that which he considered right and true. [152] I shall not say a word about Todt; from the very start he was demoralized by the contradiction between his position of yesterday and that of today, and several times he saved himself by fleeing. But I must say a word about Tzschirner. Tzschirner was recognized by everyone as the head of the democratic party in Saxony; he was the instigator, the preparer, and the leader of the revolution—and he ran at the first threat of danger; he ran, moreover, because he was frightened by a false, empty rumor. In a word, he showed himself before everyone, friends and enemies, to be a coward and a scoundrel. Later he reappeared, but I was ashamed even to speak with him, and from that time on I turned more to Heubner, whom I had come to like and respect with all my heart. The Poles also disappeared; they probably thought they should save themselves for the Polish fatherland. Henceforth I did not associate with a single Pole. This was my last farewell to the Polish nationality.

But I have interrupted my story. So Heubner and I went to the barricades, partly to hearten the fighters and partly to find out at least something about the state of affairs, concerning which no one in the room of the Provisional Government had even the slightest information. When we returned, they told us that Tzschirner and the Poles, frightened by a false alarm, had considered it necessary to leave, and advised us to do the same. Heubner decided to stay, and I also. Then Tzschirner returned, and then Todt, but the latter remained only a short time and again disappeared.

I remained, not because I hoped for success. Everything was so ruined by Messrs. Tzschirner and Heinze that only a miracle could save the democrats. There was no possibility of restoring order; everything was so confused that no one knew what to do or where or to whom to turn. I expected defeat and I remained, partly because I could not bring myself to leave poor Heubner, who was sitting there like a lamb led to the slaughter, but even more because as a Russian I was more subject than all the others to vile suspicions, and, having been slandered more than once, I felt bound, just as did Heubner, to endure to the end.

I cannot, Sire, give you a detailed account of the three or four days I spent in Dresden after the flight of the Poles. I rushed about a lot, gave advice, gave orders, constituted the whole Provisional Government almost alone; in a word, I did all I could to save the ruined and obviously dying revolution. I did not sleep, I did not eat, I did not drink, I did not even smoke. I exerted myself to the utmost and could not leave the government room for even a minute for fear that Tzschirner might run away again and leave my Heubner alone. Several times I brought together the commanders of the barricades, tried to restore order and collect forces for offensive actions. But Heinze wrecked all my undertakings in embryo, so that all my intense, feverish activity was in vain. Some of the communist leaders at the barricades thought of setting fire to Dresden, and they did burn down several houses. I never gave orders for this; I would have agreed even to this, however, if I had only thought it was possible to save the Saxon revolution by fires. I could never understand why one should feel sorrier for houses and inanimate objects than for people. The Saxon as well as Prussian soldiers amused themselves by shooting at innocent women looking out of windows, and no one was surprised at this; but when the democrats, for their own defense, began to set fire to houses, everybody began to scream about barbarism. But one must say that the good, moral, educated German soldiers demonstrated incomparably more barbarism in Dresden than did the democrats. I myself was a witness of the indignation with which all the democrats, simple people, threw themselves upon a man who took it into his head to berate some wounded Prussian soldiers. But woe to that democrat who fell into the hands of the soldiers! Messieurs the officers seldom showed themselves, watched out for themselves with the greatest tenderness, but ordered the soldiers not to take prisoners, with the result that the soldiers in the houses they seized beat up, bayoneted, and shot many people who had not even thought of mixing in the revolution; thus was stabbed, together with his valet, a young *Fürst,** apparently a relative of one of the minor German potentates, who had come to Dresden to have his eyes treated.† I learned of these circumstances not from the democrats but from a most reliable source, namely, from the noncommissioned officers who had actively participated in the Dresden events and had then been assigned to guard me. I was on most friendly terms with some of them, and in the Königstein Fortress I learned from them much that says little for the benevolence or the courage or the intelligence of Messieurs the Saxon and Prussian officers. But I shall return to my story.

I did not order the fires, but neither did I permit the city to be handed over to the troops under the pretext of putting out the fires. When it became apparent that it was no longer possi-

* Prince.
† This was Prince Schwarzburg-Rudolphstadt, according to Steklov.

ble to hold out in Dresden, I proposed to the Provisional Government that it blow itself up together with the town hall, for which I had enough gunpowder; but they did not want to.[153] Tzschirner again fled, and from that time I saw him no more. Heubner and I, having sent out everywhere the orders for a general retreat, waited a little while longer until our orders were carried out, and then left with all the militia, taking with us all the gunpowder, all the ammunition at hand, and our wounded. To this day I do not understand how we were able, how we were allowed, to carry out not a rout but a regular, orderly withdrawal, when it would have been so easy to crush us into dust in the open field. I might think that benevolence stopped the commanders of the troops if, after what I saw and heard before and after my imprisonment, I could have faith in their benevolence; and I explain this circumstance again by the fact that everything is relative in this world, and that German troops, just like German governments, were created to fight against German democrats.

Although our withdrawal was accomplished in a quite orderly fashion, however, our army was completely demoralized. Arriving in Freiburg and wishing to continue the war on the Bohemian border—I was still hoping for a Bohemian insurrection—we tried to hearten our army and to establish new order in it. But this was impossible; everyone was weary and exhausted, without any belief in success. And we ourselves kept going somehow, with our last effort, our last painful exertion. In Chemnitz, instead of the aid we expected, we found treachery; the reactionary citizens seized us at night in our beds and transported us to Altenburg to hand us over to the Prussian army. The Saxon Commission of Inquiry was later astonished that I had permitted myself to be seized, that I had not made an effort to free myself.[154] And in reality it would have been possible to break out of the hands of the burghers; but I was exhausted, drained not only physically but even more so morally, and was completely indifferent to what happened to me; only, on the way, I destroyed my pocket notebook and hoped that, following the example of Robert Blum, they would shoot me in a few days in Vienna.[155] And I feared only one thing: to be handed over to the Russian government. My hope was not realized; fate had in store for me a different lot.

In this manner did my empty, useless, and criminal life end; and it only remains for me to thank God for stopping me in time on the broad road to all crimes.

My confession is finished, Sire! It has relieved my soul. I have tried to put down in it all my sins and not forget anything essential; if I have forgotten anything, it was not on purpose. Everything in the depositions, accusations, and denunciations against me that is contrary to what I have said here is definitely false or erroneous or slanderous.

And now I turn again to my Sovereign, and, falling at the feet of Your Imperial Majesty, I implore you:

Sire! I am a great criminal and do not deserve forgiveness! I know this, and if I were sentenced to death I would accept it as a fitting punishment, I would accept it almost with joy: it would deliver me from an unbearable and intolerable existence. But Count Orlov told me, on behalf of Your Imperial Majesty, that capital punishment does not exist in Russia. I implore you, Sire, if it is possible under the law, and if a criminal's plea can touch the heart of Your Imperial Majesty, Sire, do not order me to rot in eternal fortress imprisonment! Do not punish me with a German punishment for my German sins. If the most harsh penal servitude be my lot, I shall accept it with gratitude as a kindness; the heavier the labor, the more easily will I lose myself in it! But in solitary confinement you remember everything and remember it to no avail; and your thought and your memory become an inexpressible torment, and you live long, you live against your will, and, never dying, you die every day in inactivity and anguish of loneliness. Nowhere have I been so well off, neither in the Königstein Fortress nor in Austria, as I am here in the Peter and Paul Fortress; and may God grant that any free man might find such a kind, such a humane commander as I have found here, to my great joy! And despite this, if I were given the choice I believe I would prefer not only death but even corporal punishment to eternal fortress imprisonment.

Another request, Sire! Permit me, alone and for the last time, to see and take leave of my family; if not all of them, then at least my old father and my mother and my favorite sister (I do not even know whether she is alive).*

Grant me these two greatest kindnesses, Most Gracious Sovereign, and I shall bless the providence that freed me from the hands of the Germans in order to commit me into the paternal hands of Your Imperial Majesty.

Having lost the right to call myself a loyal subject of Your Imperial Majesty, I subscribe myself with a sincere heart

The repentant sinner

MIKHAIL BAKUNIN

* Tatiana Aleksandrovna is the sister to whom Bakunin refers. Concerning Bakunin's request, Nicholas wrote: "I agree to his meeting with his father and sister in the presence of G[eneral] Nabokov [commandant of the Peter and Paul Fortress]."

NOTES

Introduction

1. A. N. Kornilov, *Gody stranstvii Mikhaila Bakunina* (Leningrad and Moscow, 1925); M. A. *Bakunin: Sobranie sochinenii i pisem, 1828–1876,* ed. Iu. M. Steklov, 4 vols., vol. IV: *V tiur'makh i ssylke, 1848–1861* (1935; reprint Düsseldorf and Vaduz, 1970); cited hereafter as Steklov.

2. Cited in E. H. Carr, *Michael Bakunin* (New York, 1961), p. 69.

3. Bakunin to Herzen, Irkutsk, 8 December 1860, in *Michail Bakunins Sozial-politischer Briefwechsel mit Alexander Iw. Herzen und Ogarjow,* ed. M. P. Dragomanov (Stuttgart, 1895), p. 35; and Steklov, IV, 366.

4. Dragomanov, *Bakunins Sozial-politischer Briefwechsel,* pp. 35–36; and Steklov, IV, 366.

5. See Steklov, IV, 417–418.

6. Bakunin to Herzen, 8 December 1860, in Dragomanov, *Bakunins Sozial-politischer Briefwechsel,* p. 37; and Steklov, IV, 367.

7. Cited in Carr, *Bakunin,* p. 304.

8. This episode is examined in Iu. M. Steklov, *Mikhail Aleksandrovich Bakunin, ego zhizn' i deiatel'nost', 1814–1876,* 4 vols., 2nd ed. (Moscow, 1926–1927), I, 256–262.

9. Notably Kurt Kersten in his introduction to *Michael Bakunins Beichte aus der Peter-Pauls-Festung an Zar Nikolaus I* (1926; reprint Frankfurt, 1973), p. 25.

10. Especially Max Nettlau, "Bakunin und seine Beichte," in the anarchist anthology *Unser Bakunin* (Berlin, 1926), p. 39.

11. It is nonetheless difficult to accept Nettlau's contention, stated elsewhere, that "four Tsars respected the 'secret of the confessional' and did not use the document against the living Bakunin, their open

enemy, or against his memory" ("Bakunin's so-called 'Confession' of 1851," *Freedom*, no. 390 *[December 1921]*, p. 75).

12. "Mikhail Aleksandrovich Bakunin, iz moikh vospominanii," *Minuvshie gody*, no. 10 (1908), pp. 148–149.

13. " 'Die Beichte' M. A. Bakunins," in *Unser Bakunin*. Sazhin's "selective memory" is vigorously challenged in Steklov, IV, 419.

14. Nettlau, "Bakunin's so-called 'Confession,' " p. 75.

15. Dragomanov, *Bakunins Sozial-politischer Briefwechsel*, p. lxiii.

16. Schiemann recorded his find in *Russische Köpfe* (1916; 2nd ed., Berlin, 1919), pp. 190–192. Orlov's letters to Nicholas are reprinted in Kersten's introduction to *Bakunins Beichte*, pp. 12–13.

17. See especially Steklov, IV, 432–433.

18. L. Il'inskii, "Ispoved' M. A. Bakunina," *Vestnik literatury*, no. 10 (1919).

19. *Ispoved' i pis'mo Aleksandru II*, ed. V. Polonskii (Moscow, 1921).

20. *Materialy dlia biografii M. Bakunina*, ed. Viacheslav Polonskii, 3 vols. (Moscow and Petrograd/Leningrad, 1923–1933), I, 100–248.

21. See n. 9.

22. *Zpověd' caru Mikuláši I*, trans. V. Charvát (Prague, 1926).

23. *Confession*, trans. P. Brupbacher (1932; reprint Paris, 1974). A new French translation by Andrée Robel is in Jacques Duclos, *Bakounine et Marx: Ombre et Lumière* (Paris, 1974), pp. 341–454.

24. Brief excerpts are translated by Valentine Snow in *The Great Prisoners*, ed. Isidore Abramowitz (New York, 1946), pp. 625–643. A Polish translation is *Michaił Bakunin, Pisma Wybrane*, ed. H. Temkinowa, 2 vols. (Warsaw; 1965), I, 399–594; a Dutch version by Arthur Lehning is forthcoming.

25. Steklov, IV, 99–207, with extensive annotation on pp. 415–551.

26. Peter Scheibert, *Von Bakunin zu Lenin: Geschichte der russischen revolutionären Ideologien 1840–1895* (Leiden, 1956), I, 326.

27. Victor Serge in *Bulletin Communiste*, no. 56 (22 December 1921); *Forum*, June 1921, pp. 373–380.

28. Notably in the English anarchist journal *Freedom*, no. 390 (December 1921), pp. 75–76; no. 395 (May 1922), pp. 28–29; and no. 416 (March–April 1924), pp. 18–19. Serge, Nettlau maintained, was now seeking to accomplish what Marx had tried unsuccessfully to do in 1848 and again in 1872: "to kill Bakunin morally."

29. *Der Anarchismus von Proudhon zu Kropotkin* (Berlin, 1927), p. 34n.

30. Polonskii, "Mikhail Bakunin v epokhu sorokovykh-shestidesiatykh godov," *Ispoved' i pis'mo Aleksandru II*, pp. 5–44.

31. "Ispoved' M. A. Bakunina," *Zadruga*, I, no. 1 (December 1921), 4–6.

32. *Vestnik truda*, II, no. 9 (1921), 152–157.

33. Carr, *Bakunin*, p. 278. The pamphlet is reprinted in Dragomanov, *Bakunins Sozial-politischer Briefwechsel*, pp. 303 ff.

34. Steklov first expressed this view in 1920, in the first edition of his multivolume biography of Bakunin (not available to this writer). He repeated his opinion in the second edition (1926–1927), noting that the discovery of letters that Bakunin had smuggled to his family in 1854 (see n. 37) only confirmed his earlier opinion and the error of those who believed in Bakunin's sincerity (Steklov, *Bakunin, ego zhizn' i deiatel'nost'*, I, 422–423; see also Steklov, IV, 423).

35. See *Pochin*, nos. 4–5 (1921–1922).

36. Kornilov, *Gody stranstvii Mikhaila Bakunina*, pp. 490 ff.

37. See Polonskii, "Michael Bakunin und seine 'Beichte,' " in Kersten, *Bakunins Beichte*, pp. 28–45. The belief that the letters to Tatiana constituted the "key" to the *Confession* was echoed by Kersten in his Introduction, pp. 9–27.

38. E.g., Max Nettlau, "A Last Word on Bakunin's 'Confession,' " *Freedom*, no. 429 (September 1925), pp. 42–43.

39. E.g., Polonskii, "Bakunin und seine 'Beichte,' " pp. 28–31; and Hélène Iswolsky, *La vie de Bakounine* (Paris, 1930), who notes (p. 145): "It was the psychological moment that the Tsar had been awaiting in order to intervene."

40. "Ispoved' M. A. Bakunina," *Zapiski Russkago Istoricheskago Obshchestva v Prage*, II (1930), 124.

41. The preceding paragraphs owe much to Jan Kucharzewski, "Spowiedź Bakunina," *Przegląd współczesny*, IV (1925), 219 ff.; Polonskii, "Bakunin und seine 'Beichte,' " pp. 28–45; and Carr, *Bakunin*, pp. 221–228.

42. Polonskii, "Bakunin und seine 'Beichte,' " pp. 43–45.

43. Bakunin to Herzen, 8 December 1860. Dragomanov, *Bakunins Sozial-politischer Briefwechsel*, p. 36; and Steklov, IV, 366.

44. Dragomanov, *Bakunins Sozial-politischer Breifwechsel*, p. 36; and Steklov, IV, 367.

45. The petition was printed in Steklov's 1920 work on Bakunin and in Polonskii's edition of the *Confession* (1921), and reprinted in Polonskii's *Materialy*, I, 284 ff. See also Steklov, IV, 272–276. Although Bakunin did not refer to this second "confession" in his letter to Herzen, in a letter to his brother Aleksei, 23 February 1857, he wrote: "Three days ago I received through the commandant here the

announcement that the Sovereign Emperor, touched by my repentance and deigning to concede to my plea, has most graciously been pleased to mitigate my punishment by . . . exile . . . to Siberia" (Steklov, IV, 278).

46. Alexander Herzen, *From the Other Shore* (London, 1956); Friedrich Engels, *Germany: Revolution and Counter-Revolution*, in *The German Revolutions*, ed. Leonard Krieger (Chicago, 1967).

Confession

1. Count Aleksei Fedorovich Orlov (1786–1861) in 1844 succeeded Count A. K. Benckendorff as head of the Third Section of the Imperial Chancellery.

2. Herzen (see n. 52) describes Bakunin's brief military career differently: "Having completed the course in the artillery corps, Bakunin was graduated as a guards officer. They say that his father, angry at him, requested that he be transferred to the army. Abandoned in some godforsaken Belorussian village with his military unit, Bakunin shunned society, became unsocial, did not carry out his duties, and lay on his bed for days on end in a sheepskin coat. The commander of his unit was sorry for him but had no alternative but to remind him that it was necessary for him either to carry out his duties or go into retirement. Bakunin had not suspected that he had this right, and immediately asked to be retired" (A. I. Gertsen, *Byloe i dumy*, 2 vols. [Moscow, 1962], I, 370).

3. Frederick William IV's accession to the Prussian throne in 1840 raised the hopes of the German liberals. The new monarch was an incurable romantic, however, and he soon showed that his idea of reform was the Christian paternalism of medieval times.

4. Arnold Ruge (1802–1880) was a radical publicist whose journals—*Hallische Jahrbücher* (1838–1841) and *Deutsche Jahrbücher* (Dresden, 1841–1843)—were the principal organs of the Young Hegelian left.

5. Lorenz von Stein (1815–1890) was an advocate of the ideas of Saint-Simon. His book *Der Sozialismus und Kommunismus des heutigen Frankreichs* introduced the early socialist currents in France to the German democrats.

6. In his *Life of Jesus* (1835–1836), David Friedrich Strauss (1808–1874) challenged the credibility of the Gospels as historical evidence. This book was a turning point in the critical study of early Christianity and anticipated the writings of Ernest Renan and Albert

Schweitzer. Public opposition to Strauss's theories prevented him from accepting a teaching position at the University of Zurich in 1839.

7. Bakunin's article, actually entitled "Die Reaktion in Deutschland," closed with the celebrated passage: "Let us therefore trust in the eternal spirit that destroys and annihilates only because it is the unfathomable and eternally creative source of all life. The desire for destruction is also a creative desire."

8. Georg Herwegh (1817–1875) published *Poems of a Living Man* (1841) in Zurich. The book gained the young poet a wide following and made him the darling of the German democrats.

9. Julius Fröbel (1805–1893), German émigré, went to Zurich in 1833 and taught mineralogy there for several years before devoting himself entirely to radical politics. Returning to Germany, he was elected to the Frankfurt Parliament in 1848, and in October of that year he barely escaped execution (the fate of his radical associate Robert Blum) for his part in the abortive Viennese insurrection.

10. Friedrich Rhomer (1814–1856) was a reactionary Zurich lawyer who succumbed to megalomania in 1841 and presented himself as a new messiah. Theodor Rhomer (1816–1856), the "prophet" and a romantic mystic, proclaimed his brother's mission to regenerate the Germanic nation by the tight union of church and state.

11. Wilhelm Weitling (1808–1871) had fled Germany to avoid military conscription. He studied socialism and revolutionary tactics in France, but when he was implicated in the Blanquist putsch attempt in 1839, he took refuge in Switzerland. The impending publication of *The Gospel of a Poor Sinner*, which depicted Christ as a communist rebel and the illegitimate son of Mary (with remarkable parallels to Weitling's own illegitimacy), led to Weitling's arrest by Zurich authorities in June 1843.

12. After Weitling's arrest he was sentenced to ten months in prison for blasphemy and covert communist propaganda. In 1844 he was handed over to the Prussian government, which soon released him. Weitling went to London, then to Brussels, and finally to America (M. A. Bakunin. *Sobranie sochinenii i pisem, 1828–1876*, ed. Iu. M. Steklov, 4 vols., vol. IV: *V tiur'makh i ssylke, 1848–1861* [1935; reprint Düsseldorf and Vaduz, 1970]; cited hereafter as Steklov).

13. Johann Bluntschli's report, which mentioned Bakunin as one of Weitling's accomplices, was published on 21 July 1843. Four days later the Russian legation in Bern asked the Swiss authorities for further information on Bakunin's activities, a request to which the Swiss

readily acceded. These and subsequent reports communicated to Petersburg by A. I. Struve led to an official summons, on 6 February 1844, for Bakunin to return to Russia. His refusal precipitated the first of his trials *in absentia*. In December 1844, by the tsar's decree, he was deprived of his military rank and gentry status and was sentenced to banishment in Siberia for an indefinite period.

14. As Steklov (IV, 436) points out, Bakunin knew that, in the eyes of Nicholas I, relations with Poles were a particularly serious offense. Here Bakunin tells a falsehood, for it had been proposed that he write a book about Russia. There probably was no question at this time of a pamphlet on Poland. It is doubtful that he had no Polish acquaintances or that he met no Poles in Dresden.

15. Adolph Reichel, German musician, is remembered solely because of his intimate friendship with Bakunin. Reichel and his Russian wife, although not involved in Bakunin's political imbroglios, remained his loyal friends. The Reichels were present at Bakunin's deathbed in Bern on 1 July 1876.

16. Joachim Lelewel (1786–1861), Polish historian and democratic politician, was active in the unsuccessful November 1830 Polish insurrection against tsarist rule.

17. "Little Russia" (Malorossiia) was the official tsarist designation for the Ukraine. The term first appeared in fourteenth-century ecclesiastical documents to distinguish the former Kievan Rus' diocese from the Muscovite (Great Russian) diocese. Not until the end of the nineteenth century did the term "Little Russian" acquire a distinctly pejorative connotation (much as "Ruthene" was used for Ukrainian in Austrian Galicia). At mid-century democratic and conservative Poles still viewed the peoples of Poland's former eastern territories—White Russians and Ukrainians—as *gente Rutheni, natione Poloni* (Ruthenian people of the Polish nation).

18. The address in question was delivered on 26 November 1831, the first anniversary of the Polish insurrection. Later published as *Discours de M. J. Lelewel* (Paris, 1832), this and other appeals to the French Chamber of Deputies and to other governments called on the Russian people to make common cause with other nations against tsarist tyranny. Lelewel's outspokenness led to protests from the Russian ambassador, Count Carlo Andrea Pozzo di Borgo, and Lelewel was expelled from Paris by Louis Philippe's conservative government. Lelewel lived briefly in Tours before finding sanctuary in Brussels. Continuing to associate with leftist émigrés, he devoted himself chiefly to historical study.

19. Bakunin had visited Paris briefly in March 1844 at the invitation of a family acquaintance.

20. The *Deutsch-Französische Jahrbücher* was edited by Arnold Ruge and Karl Marx. It was at this time that Bakunin first became acquainted with Marx and Engels. A reprint edition of the *Jahrbücher* was published in Leipzig in 1973.

21. After the *Jahrbücher* failed, Marx and Ruge contributed for a short time to the weekly German-language *Vorwärts* in Paris. Their quarrels annoyed Bakunin, who was obviously pleased when, at the request of the Russian government, the French authorities closed down *Vorwärts* and expelled Marx in January 1845.

22. After brief service in the Russian diplomatic corps, Ivan Gavrilovich Golovin (1816–1886) emigrated to Western Europe, where he wrote numerous pamphlets and books criticizing the tsarist system. The Parisian legal chronicle *Gazette des tribunaux* had reprinted on 16 January 1845 the official Russian communiqué of the sentences against Bakunin and Golovin. In a letter to the editor published two days later, Golovin denounced Nicholas' action as a violation of privileges granted to the Russian nobility by several Romanov rulers.

23. In the letter, published in *La Réforme*, 27 January 1845, Bakunin railed against Golovin's naïve underestimation of the tsar's absolute power and its ruthless exercise. But despite the government's brutality, Bakunin believed that the Russian people had remained instinctively democratic and uncorrupted, and he foresaw a time when the tide of revolutionary unrest would bring freedom to Russia.

24. Prince Adam Jerzy Czartoryski (1770–1861), leader of the conservative wing of the Polish emigration, dispatched agents throughout Europe to work for Poland's restitution from his headquarters at the Hôtel Lambert on the Île Saint-Louis. To his admirers, Czartoryski was the uncrowned king of Poland.

25. Kondratii Fedorovich Ryleev (1795–1826) and Pavel Ivanovich Pestel (1799–1826) were two of the five leaders of the Decembrist (1825) uprising who were executed. The invitation to the ceremony honoring them was sent to Bakunin on 19 April 1845 by the Polish émigré Karol B. Stolzman (1793–1854). Bakunin later sent the original of this letter to his sister Tatiana at Priamukhino. He may have referred to this invitation under the assumption that the authorities had it in their possession.

26. Alojzy Biernacki (1778–1854), liberal Polish landowner and agronomist, was finance minister in the 1831 revolutionary government. He tried unsuccessfully to have compulsory serf labor con-

verted to rent payments. After the Polish insurrection failed, Biernacki emigrated to France.

Nikolai Ivanovich Turgenev (1789–1871), Russian writer and official, was an associate of the Decembrists. He had evaded capture and now lived in Paris.

27. Adam Mickiewicz (1798–1855), illustrious Polish poet and revolutionary whose romantic verse kept alive the dreams of Polish émigrés for their country's resurrection, was appointed to the chair of Slavic literatures at the Collège de France in 1840.

28. Andrzej Towiański (1799–1878), Polish mystic whose messianism, which envisaged a new community of chosen nations guided by true Christian principles, exerted a compelling attraction on Mickiewicz in the early 1840s.

29. Michel-Auguste Chambolle (1802–1883) was appointed editor in chief of the liberal Paris daily Le Siècle in 1837. A member of the Chamber of Deputies from 1838, he was reelected to the Legislative Assembly in 1848 as a moderate republican. His opposition to Louis Napoleon led to his arrest and brief exile after the coup d'état of 2 December 1851.

Charles Merruau (1807–?), a political associate of Adolphe Thiers, edited the liberal Le Constitutionnel from 1844 to 1849.

Emile de Girardin (1806–1881) on 1 July 1836 founded the Paris daily La Presse. He was able to sell subscriptions at half the price of competing newspapers because the increased circulation attracted advertisers whose payments offset the loss of income resulting from the lower price per copy. Girardin began his career as a supporter of the July Monarchy, but his critical journalistic style soon earned the enmity of the Orléanist regime.

Xavier Durrieu (1814–1868) was successively contributor to Le Siècle and editor in chief of Le Temps before transferring in 1845 to the Paris daily Le Courrier français, which under Durrieu's influence became the leading organ of the radical opposition to the July Monarchy. In 1848 he and Auguste Blanqui founded the first revolutionary club. Durrieu was arrested and expelled from France after Louis Napoleon's coup d'état.

The economists Léon Faucher (1803–1854), Claude-Frédéric Bastiat (1801–1850), and Louis Wolowski (1810–1876) held moderate republican views and were staunch proponents of free trade policies and disciples of Adam Smith. In 1846 Bastiat founded the Association pour la liberté des échanges and propounded his antiprotectionist views in the pages of its journal, *Le Libre-échange*. During 1848–1849 he attacked the socialists, whom he identified with protectionism. Faucher and his brother-in-law Wolowski, a refugee of the 1830 Polish insurrection and a naturalized French citizen, founded the Crédit Foncier in 1852.

Pierre-Jean de Béranger (1780–1857) was a poet and songwriter whose liberal, patriotic, and anticlerical lyrics earned him an immense following.

Félicité-Robert de Lamennais (1782–1854), priest and publicist, founded (with Count Charles de Montalembert) the journal *L'Avenir*, which attempted to fuse political liberalism and Roman Catholicism. Lamennais opposed Gallicanism, but his radical Ultramontane views displeased Pope Gregory XVI, who denounced Catholic liberalism in his encyclical *Mirari Vos* (1832).

François Arago (1786–1853), physicist and astronomer, who discovered the principle that magnetism is induced by rotation and devised an experiment to prove the wave theory of light. An ardent republican, he was minister of war and marine in the 1848 Provisional Government.

Etienne Arago (1802–1892), younger brother of François, was active in the Carbonari and other radical societies. A cofounder of the radical *La Réforme*, Etienne was appointed postal director in the Provisional Government with the task of assuring communication between republican Paris and the provinces. As mayor of Paris in 1870, he prepared the city's defenses against the Prussians, but he did not join the Commune.

Emmanuel Arago (1812–1896), son of François and nephew of Etienne, was a lawyer who defended in court the radical opponents of the July Monarchy.

The republican journalist Armand Marrast (1801–1852) successively edited *La Tribune* and *Le National* and was active in the banquet campaign that preceded the fall of Louis Philippe. He was mayor of Paris in 1848, but sided with the moderates after the June Days.

Jules Bastide (1800–1879) preceded Marrast as editor of *Le National*. He is credited with persuading Lamartine to declare the Republic in February 1848. In May of that year he succeeded Lamartine as foreign minister and held several posts during the Second Republic.

Godefroy Cavaignac (1801–1845), an ardent democrat and leader of the republican opposition to the Bourbon restoration and the July Monarchy, was imprisoned by Louis Philippe in 1834 but escaped to

England. Granted amnesty in 1841, he wrote for *La Réforme* and in 1843 became president of the Society of the Rights of Man.

Ferdinand Flocon (1800–1866) served for a time as editor in chief of *La Réforme* and was later minister of commerce in the Provisional Government. He was exiled following Louis Napoleon's coup d'état.

Louis Blanc (1811–1882), utopian socialist, radical journalist, and historian, was a member of the Provisional Government. His socialist program, outlined in his *L'Organisation du travail* (1840), envisaged the establishment of workers' associations (*ateliers sociaux*) organized by trades to govern production. After the suppression of the June insurrection in Paris, Blanc found refuge in England.

After Charles Fourier's death in 1837, Victor-Prosper Considérant (1808–1893) became the leading spokesman of Fourierist utopianism and edited the theoretical journals *La Phalange* and *La Démocratie pacifique*. Forced to leave France in 1849, he founded a Fourierist community in Texas. He compiled the major theoretical work of the Fourierist school, *La Destinée sociale* (1834–1838).

Pascal Duprat (1816–1885) contributed to *La Réforme* before becoming director of *La Revue indépendante* in 1847. A moderate during the Second Republic, he opposed socialism and supported General Cavaignac's suppression of the workers' demonstrations in June 1848. He was banished after Louis Napoleon's coup d'état, but returned later to serve the Third Republic.

Félix Pyat (1810–1889), littérateur and journalist, denounced literary romanticism as politically reactionary. An outspoken radical in the Jacobin (not Marxist) tradition, he supported the June 1848 uprising and was forced to live abroad until 1869. A member of the Paris Commune, he again was forced to flee when the Commune fell. He was finally granted amnesty in 1880.

Victor Schoelcher (1804–1893) traveled in France's colonies and became a firm abolitionist. As a member of the Provisional Government he drafted the law emancipating the slaves. After Louis Napoleon seized power, Schoelcher fled to England.

Jules Michelet (1798–1874), the distinguished and prolific historian of the romanticist-national school, is most noted for his monumental multivolume *Histoire de France* (1833–1867), whose thesis is France's historical mission as the champion of democracy.

Edgar Quinet (1803–1875), philosopher and historian, was a professor at the Collège de France. His anticlericalism and his exaltation of the Great French Revolution displeased the government and cost him his professorship in 1846. Quinet supported the Second Republic but was forced to flee after Louis Napoleon's coup d'état.

Pierre-Joseph Proudhon (1809–1865), the utopian socialist, was from an impoverished peasant background. His program of mutualist economic organization and opposition to political centralism was the foundation of anarchist theory. Although Bakunin termed Proudhon a "utopian" in the *Confession*, he later acknowledged Proudhon's paramount influence on his own political development.

George Sand was the pen name of Amandine Aurore Lucie Dudevant, *née* Dupin (1804–1876). A prolific romantic novelist whose notorious love affairs, notably with Chopin and Musset, and her advocacy of social equality for women placed her in the forefront of European intellectual life.

30. Terenzio Mamiani della Rovere (1799–1885), an Italian writer, lived in Paris after taking part in the unsuccessful insurrection of 1831 in Bologna. Guglielmo Pepe (1783–1855) was a Neapolitan general associated with the Carbonari in Italy.

31. See n. 39.

32. Adolphe Thiers (1797–1877), French premier under Louis Philippe in 1840, pursued an aggressive foreign policy that brought Europe to the brink of war. When his support of the Egyptian ruler Mehemet Ali against the Ottoman sultan was countered by the other European powers, Thiers threatened to attack the Rhineland. War was averted when Louis Philippe replaced Thiers with his political rival, François Guizot.

33. Louis Philippe (1773–1850), Duke of Orléans, acceded to the throne in the July 1830 revolution, backed by the liberal opponents of the Bourbon restoration. His middle-class support and outlook caused his reign to be dubbed the "bourgeois monarchy." His headlong flight in February 1848 triggered the spread of revolution in Europe.

34. Friends of Light (Lichtfreunde), a movement founded in 1841 by German Protestants who sought to return to simple Christian virtue and to end religious obscurantism, was banned by the Prussian government in 1845. The German Catholic movement (Deutschkatholizismus) began as a protest against an exhibition in Trier in 1844 of the so-called Holy Cloak. Its leader, Johannes Ronge, denounced the exhibition as a "modern indulgence racket." Although excommunicated, Ronge and his fellow Silesian Johannes Czerski founded several "free congregations" that rejected papal authority, used the ver-

nacular in the liturgy, abolished confession, permitted priests to marry, and espoused a form of primitive socialism.

35. After years of conspiring, Polish émigrés planned simultaneous insurrections for February 1846 in their partitioned homeland. In Poznań the plot was betrayed and the conspirators were rounded up by the Prussian authorities, while in the Congress Kingdom and in western Galicia the peasantry turned against the "liberating" Polish nobles. Only in the free city of Kraków did the insurgents hold out for a time.

36. Bakunin's article of 19 March 1846 devoted particular attention to the persecution and "Russification" of the Uniate church in the former Polish eastern territories by Orthodox tsarist officialdom.

37. "Centralizacja" denoted the five-man executive board of the Polish Democratic Society, founded in 1832 in France by Poles who had emigrated after the November 1830 insurrection. The society was the principal rival to Czartoryski's conservative wing of the Polish emigration.

38. The Polish émigrés, with bitter memories of Russian oppression, probably found it difficult to trust any Russian, especially one as flamboyant as Bakunin. And Bakunin could offer the Poles little but grandiose schemes. Though his services were refused by the Centralizacja, Bakunin continued to frequent Polish circles in Paris.

39. In his banquet address Bakunin urged the reconciliation of Poles and Russians and their liberation from "foreign" despotism (an allusion to Tsar Nicholas' German ancestry). In this, his first major public address, Bakunin dazzled the audience with his oratory. Even before the speech appeared in *La Réforme* on 17 December 1847, the Russian minister, Nikolai Kiselev, protested Bakunin's slander of the Russian government. To pacify the Russians, the French authorities summarily expelled Bakunin, who, unlike the Polish émigrés, lacked political influence.

40. This speech of 14 February 1848 has not been preserved. Bakunin and Lelewel spoke at a ceremony commemorating the fallen Russian revolutionaries, and in particular Szymon Konarski, the Polish revolutionary executed by tsarist authorities in Wilno in 1839.

41. François Guizot (1787–1874), French statesman and historian, was minister in several cabinets under the July Monarchy. He dominated French politics during the 1840s, but not until 1847—on the eve of the February Revolution—did Louis Philippe formally appoint him prime minister.

42. As early as 6 February 1847, the Paris police reported that

rumors that Bakunin was a tsarist spy were circulating among the Polish émigrés. Not satisfied with Bakunin's expulsion from Paris, Kiselev planted a rumor that Bakunin had served the Russians as an *agent provocateur* but had outlived his usefulness. The ambassador obviously hoped to drive a further wedge between Bakunin and the Poles. The French minister of the interior, Count Charles Duchâtel, may have characterized Bakunin as a petty criminal in order to deflect criticism of Bakunin's expulsion among the French government's opponents. Although Bakunin repeatedly denied these accusations, rumors continued to harass him as he followed the path of revolution across Europe in the spring of 1848. The origin and dissemination of the various charges are examined in Josef Pfitzner, *Bakuninstudien* (Prague, 1932), especially chaps. 2–4.

43. There were two communist societies in Brussels at this time: the internationally oriented Democratic Association, to which Bakunin belonged for a brief time, and the German Workers Union (Deutsche Arbeiter Verein). Both were strongly influenced by Marx, who had made Brussels the center of his communist schemes after his expulsion from Paris in 1845. Bakunin's contempt for the German communists is also evident in his letters to Herwegh and Pavel Vasil'evich Annenkov (1812–1887), a Russian literary critic who lived abroad.

44. General Jan Skrzynecki (1787–1860), a conservative Polish émigré, commanded the Polish forces during part of the 1831 campaign against Russia.

Count Philippe de Mérode (1791–1857), a conservative Belgian statesman, served Leopold I in various ministerial and ambassadorial posts after Belgium was granted independence in 1830.

Count Charles de Montalembert (1810–1870), an associate of Lamennais, with whom he founded *L'Avenir,* championed the separation of church and state in educational matters.

Although Mérode, Montalembert, and Lamennais all held Ultramontane views, Bakunin's reference to "Jesuitic propaganda" is purely figurative.

45. Marc Caussidière (1808–1861), police chief of revolutionary Paris, organized the Garde du peuple, a militia largely made up of former prisoners, to replace the detested Municipal Guard of the July Monarchy. To Caussidière is attributed the celebrated remark concerning Bakunin's first encounter with revolution: "What a man! On the first day of the revolution he was priceless; on the second he should have been shot."

46. The anarchist and Bakunin scholar Max Nettlau, commenting on the preceding pages, maintained that "This veritable poem to Paris of the February barricades . . . , sung in the face of the Tsar" should put to rest the insinuations that Bakunin had abased himself before the tsar and compromised himself by writing the *Confession* (notes to the French edition of the *Confession* [1932; reprint Paris, 1974], p. 218; hereafter cited as Nettlau).

47. In a letter of 17 March 1850 to Franz Otto, his attorney at the Dresden trial, Bakunin emphasized this distinction between the Russian people and their rulers: "After the outbreak of revolution in Paris, Vienna, and Berlin, everyone expected a general war of liberated Europe against Russia. . . . At that time, nothing was spoken about more than hurling back Russia into Asia. For me as a Russian, this was too painful. I wanted a European war, a war against the Russian government for the liberation of Poland, but not for the annihilation of the Russian people, whom I respect with all my heart" (Viacheslav Polonskii, ed., *Materialy dlia biografii M. Bakunina*, 3 vols. [Moscow and Petrograd/Leningrad, 1923–1933], I, 50).

48. Alexandre Ledru-Rollin (1807–1874), a lawyer, joined François Arago and Louis Blanc in 1843 to found *La Réforme*, the principal organ of republican opposition to the July Monarchy. Ledru-Rollin was minister of the interior in the Provisional Government.

Illustrative of this accusation is a Berlin police report of 26 July 1849, which was used at Bakunin's Dresden trial: "After the outbreak of the February Revolution in Paris, Bakunin . . . befriended Ledru-Rollin and became his emissary: (1) to stir up and republicanize areas of Slav speech, and (2) to bring about war between Prussia and Russia" (in Kurt Kersten, ed., *Michael Bakunins Beichte aus der Peter-Pauls-Festung an Zar Nikolaus I* [1926; reprint Frankfurt, 1973], p. 220).

49. Albert was the pseudonym of Alexandre Martin (1815–1895), a mechanic by trade and the only working-class representative in the Provisional Government.

50. On Bakunin's *Appeal to the Slavs*, see n. 71. There is no evidence that he wrote any articles for *La Réforme* after leaving Paris.

51. Herwegh had assumed control of the German Democratic Society in Paris, which comprised about 800 German workers. The republican government offered to pay their passage out of the country (the offer was made to all unemployed foreigners in Paris). Herwegh, a dreamer and egotistical and despotic by nature, was ill suited to command the German legionaries who assembled in Strasbourg in late March. There were incessant squabbles among the legionaries and

between them and the local authorities. Herwegh's proposal to use his men against the Danes in Schleswig-Holstein was vetoed by the Prussian government. His attempt to aid a coup in the Duchy of Baden, planned by the south German radical Friedrich Hecker and by Gustav Struve, likewise failed when the legion all but dissolved because of dissension and inadequate arms and supplies. Marx criticized Herwegh's adventurist schemes, but Bakunin rallied to his friend's defense, thus adding to the breach between Marx and Bakunin.

52. On Golovin, see n. 22.

Nikolai Ivanovich Sazonov (1815–1862), a member of a Saint-Simonist circle at Moscow University, emigrated in the early 1840s and developed close ties with Western European radicals and socialists. He was active in the 1848 upheaval and later contributed to Herzen's journal *Poliarnaia Zvezda* (The Polar Star).

Aleksandr Ivanovich Gertsen (1812–1870) was the illegitimate son of the eccentric nobleman Ivan A. Iakovlev, who gave him the surname Herzen to indicate that he was born of an affair of the heart. As a student in Moscow, Herzen devoured German romantic literature and the writings of the French utopian socialists. His radical political expressions led to his arrest and a short exile. Upon his father's death in 1847, Herzen, with a sizable inheritance, emigrated to Western Europe in time to observe the failure of the 1848 revolutions at firsthand. In 1851 he settled in England, where he undertook various publishing ventures for the purpose of enlightening Russia on the subjects of political reform and social revolution. The best known was the journal *Kolokol* (The Bell), clandestinely distributed among a wide readership. Herzen's memoirs, *Byloe i dumy* (My Past and Thoughts), is a remarkable record of his life and of the formative years of the Russian intelligentsia.

53. In his letter of 17 March 1850 to Otto (see n. 47), Bakunin wrote that, at the time he was arrested in Berlin in April 1848, he was officially informed that this accusation came from the Russian embassy. He further stated that on three occasions between May and October 1848 the Russian ambassador to Berlin used this charge as a pretext for trying to have Bakunin extradited (Polonskii, *Materialy*, I, 51).

54. Here Bakunin tries to convince the tsar of his opposition to regicide. Marcus Junius Brutus (82?–42 B.C.), desiring to re-establish the Roman Republic, was persuaded by Cassius to join the conspiracy that led to the assassination of Julius Caesar. François Ravaillac (1578–1610) assassinated Henry IV of France in the fanatical belief that

the king's policies were harmful to the Catholic Church. Louis Ali-baud (1810–1836) failed in his attempt to assassinate Louis Phillppe in 1836. Alibaud's widely publicized trial and execution were doubtless familiar to the tsar.

55. Ivan Andreevich Krylov (1768–1844), fabulist and moralist, used the vernacular to satirize human frailties, social customs, and political events. Steklov (IV, 459) states that clearly Bakunin is refer-ring to the fable "The Frog and the Ox": The Frog, envious of the size of the Ox, begins "to puff, and pant, and blow himself up." Informed by his female friend that his attempts have produced little result, the Frog continues to puff, "And my schemer ended it like this, / Unable to equal the Ox in size, / He bursts from trying—and he dies."

56. The Vorparlament (Pre-Parliament) was a self-chosen assem-blage of German liberals and democrats who met in Frankfurt on 31 March 1848 to lay the groundwork for an elective assembly to legislate German unity. It chose a Committee of Fifty to make the arrange-ments for the Frankfurt Parliament, which convened in May.

57. Bakunin expressed his troubled feeling more revealingly in a letter of 17 April 1848 to P. V. Annenkov: "The farther north I get, the sadder and more frightened I become: there, the dark power of the Russian . . ." (sentence left unfinished) (Steklov, III, 299).

58. Bakunin arrived in Berlin on 20 April, intending to leave for Breslau the following morning; but, having overslept the morning train (according to the hotel register), he visited the home of Her-wegh's father-in-law, which was under surveillance. Bakunin was ar-rested and brought before the Berlin chief of police, Baron von Minu-toli. Instead of informing the Ministry of the Interior (which would probably have notified the Foreign Ministry and thereby alerted the Russian embassy, which would surely have invoked the 1844 extradi-tion treaty with Prussia), the enigmatic Minutoli treated Bakunin as a political exile. The new passport was issued in the name of Simon, a Prussian subject from Berlin, and Minutoli then told conflicting stories to the Russian and French ambassadors, who by this time had learned of Bakunin's arrest. Bakunin's account is essentially accurate, although he fails to mention that he stopped briefly en route to Bres-lau to visit Ruge in Leipzig. Bakunin's movements in Berlin and Minutoli's actions are reconstructed in Josef Pfitzner, "Michael Ba-kunin und Preussen im Jahre 1848," *Jahresberichte für Kultur und Ge-schichte der Slaven*, VII (1931), 239–243.

59. Following the April setbacks in the Duchy of Poznań and in Kraków, Polish leaders convened in Breslau on 5 May with the aim of

coordinating the disparate elements of the Polish national struggle. Dissension between conservatives and democrats, however, and especially the reluctance of the Galician representatives to place the Lvov National Council (Rada Narodowa) under control of a superior organization, hampered attempts to mold a common program. After issuing a general manifesto, the conferees dispersed without concrete results. The congress has been studied in M. Tyrowicz, *Polski kongres polityczny w Wrocławiu 1848 r.* (Kraków, 1946).

60. Count Jan Ledóchowski (1791–1864) had emigrated after the Polish insurrection of 1830–1831. Alphonse Marie-Louis de Lamartine (1790–1869), romantic poet and historian, headed the Provisional Government after the fall of the July Monarchy and served as foreign minister. Ambassador Kiselev had probably repeated to Lamartine the same rumors about Bakunin that had worked so effectively with Guizot.

61. Bakunin learned of the congress from the Czech Slavist F. L. Čelakovský, a professor at the University of Breslau. Bakunin's British biographer E. H. Carr suggests that "in the gloom of Breslau, [the congress] was a brilliant ray of light." Bakunin journeyed to Prague with the Pole Wojciech Cybulski, a professor at the University of Berlin whose acquaintance he had made while studying there in the early 1840s. Even before the opening ceremonies, the Prague press singled out Bakunin as "one of the celebrities attending the Slav Congress" (*Bohemia*, no. 87 [1 June 1848]).

62. Cyprien Robert (1807–?) was the author of *Les Deux panslavismes* (1847) and *Le Monde slave* (1851). Closely allied with the Czartoryski conservative wing of the Polish emigration, he brought the plight and aspirations of the non-Russian Slavs to the attention of the French public in 1848–1849 in his journal *La Pologne, Journal des Slaves confédérés*.

63. František Palacký (1798–1876) was a Czech historian and political spokesman. His monumental *History of the Czech Nation*, begun in 1836, awakened in the Czechs a pride in the past glories of their nation. Palacký's refusal of 11 April 1848 to join the Frankfurt Committee of Fifty symbolized the determination of Austria's Slavs to resist inclusion of their homelands in a greater German state. In Palacký's opinion, only an independent, federally restructured, and politically reformed Austrian state could protect the smaller Danubian Slav nations, positioned between obscurantist tsardom and alien German nationalism, from absorption by Germany and Russia. Palacký's letter, the first political expression of Austro-Slavism, contained the

noteworthy passage: "If the Austrian state had not already existed for so long, it would have been in the interests of Europe, indeed of humanity itself, to endeavor to create it as soon as possible."

Pavel Josef Šafařík (1795–1861) was a Slovak-born philologist and ethnographer, whose studies of Slavic antiquities, ethnography, and literatures provided the scholarly foundations for Jan Kollár's poetic vision of a common Slavdom.

Count Josef Matyáš Thun (1794–1868), Bohemian noble and patriot, patronized the Czech national awakening before 1848 to counter the centralizing designs of the Habsburg administration. The Czechs chose Thun to chair the Preparatory Committee of the Slav Congress, but he did not actively participate in the formal congress sessions because of his imperfect command of the Czech language.

Václav Hanka (1791–1861), Czech littérateur and archivist, "discovered" two medieval manuscripts written in Czech and thereby unleashed a fierce controversy. Although present-day scholars generally regard them as forgeries, belief in their authenticity was a tenet of faith for nineteenth-century Czech intellectuals. Hanka embraced Kollár's cultural Pan-Slavism and was known as a Russophile. In 1848 he was curator of the Czech National Museum in Prague.

Jan Kollár (1793–1852) was a Slovak littérateur whose epic poem *Daughter of Sláva* (1824) enraptured Slav enthusiasts by its idyllic depiction of a glorious Slav past. His Pan-Slav treatise *On Literary Reciprocity Between the Various Branches and Dialects of the Slav Nation* (1837) presented a program for cultural sharing and mutual enrichment among all Slavs. The Magyars prevented Kollár, who was living in Budapest in 1848, from attending the Slav Congress.

Jozef Miloslav Hurban (1817–1888), Lutheran pastor and writer, was a Slovak patriot and an intimate associate of L'udovít Štúr (1815–1856), Slovak writer and national spokesman, who championed Slovak resistance to Magyarization in the 1840s. Štúr's newspaper, *Slovenskje Národňje Novini*, introduced literary language based on the Slovak vernacular. This step was opposed by the Czechs, as well as by Kollár and Šafařík, who maintained that Slovak was merely a Czech dialect, and that Czech should be the written language. Štúr was forced to flee Slovakia in the spring of 1848 because of Magyar opposition. His reconciliation with the Czechs over the issue of written Slovak paved the way for the Slav Congress.

64. Palacký, Šafařík, and J. M. Thun were largely responsible for the preparations and organization of the Prague Congress, but the idea itself originated not with the Czechs but with the Croat Ivan

Kukuljević-Saksinski and the Slovak L'udovít Štúr, who sought broad Slav support against Magyar national intolerance in their homelands. Štúr brought his proposal to Prague in late April 1848, and succeeded in winning over the Czechs. The suggestion for a Slav gathering was also made concurrently by the Poznanian Pole Jędrzej Moraczewski.

65. Count Leo Thun (1811–1888), like his cousin J. M. Thun (see n. 63), had defended the Czech and Slovak cultural aspirations in the early 1840s. He served in the Austrian administration in Galicia before his appointment in April 1848 as governor of Bohemia. As governor he was forced to share authority with the National Committee that had emerged from the March revolution. After the emperor fled to Innsbruck on May 17, Thun refused to obey the directives of the "constitutional" government in Vienna and established a sort of advisory "governing council" in Prague, whose members included Palacký and Brauner. Discredited by the June uprising, during which he was briefly held captive by the insurgents, he was replaced as governor in July.

František August Brauner (1810–1880), a Czech lawyer and political moderate, played a key role in the first days of the March revolution in Prague. Arrested by the military on suspicion of complicity in the June uprising, he was elected to the Austrian Reichstag while in prison.

66. Bakunin's chastisement of the Czech politicians is reminiscent of the dislike and mistrust that many Poles—and Bakunin associated with Poles more than anyone else in Prague—felt for the Czechs. The Poles resented not only the Czechs' preoccupation with the security and preservation of Austria (one of the partitioning powers), but the Czechs' conviction that they—a small nation compared to the Poles—were best suited to lead the Slav cause. Bakunin's allegation of Czech territorial designs is not substantiated by the evidence. On the contrary, the Czechs at the congress demurred at laying claim to either Austrian Silesia or Slovakia, while the idea of their wishing to annex Galicia is absurd. The intricacies of Polish-Czech relations in this period are admirably studied in Václav Žáček, *Čechové a Poláci roku 1848*, 2 vols. (Prague, 1947–1948).

67. On 2 June the Slav Congress convened amid pomp and euphoric outbursts of Slav sentiment. The official membership list records 340 names (the large majority Czech), though many other persons participated unofficially as guests or observers. The overriding purpose of the gathering was to achieve a common stand by the Slavs to combat German and Magyar expansionist designs. The divi-

sion of the congress into national sections was intended to avoid linguistic misunderstanding and to expedite the deliberations. The Czech organizers expected that the principal business would be conducted in the smaller executive and plenary committees, consisting of the congress officers and an equal number of representatives from each section. This plan failed to eliminate clashes among some of the participating nations, however, or to resolve differences over means and aims.

68. The priest was Alimpii Miloradov from Belaia Krinitsa, in Bukovina, the see of a Russian schismatic (Old Ritualist or Old Believer) metropolitan. The schismatic hierarchy of Belaia Krinitsa was set up and supported by powerful Old Believers in the 1840s, following the dissolution of the Old Believer monasteries by Nicholas I and the decision to forbid the Old Believers to accept "reanointed" priests from the official church. The Austrian government had agreed to the establishment of the Old Believer hierarchy in Belaia Krinitsa, where a Russian colony had long existed. Father Alimpii was in the Peter and Paul Fortress in the spring of 1854 and was transferred to Schlüsselburg with Bakunin on 12 March 1854. Bakunin apparently placed some faith in the revolutionary potential of Miloradov, whom he met again in London in 1862 (Steklov, IV, 471, 559).

Bakunin errs in attributing authorship to Šafařík. The semiofficial accounts of the congress are V. V. Tomek, [Historická] zpráwa o sjezdu slowanskem (Prague, 1848), and J. P. Jordan, Aktenmässiger Bericht über die Verhandlungen des ersten Slavenkongresses in Prag (Prague, 1848).

69. Bakunin's recollection of his speech is remarkably similar to the version recorded in the protocol of the session: "[Russian] affairs are closely tied to the Polish question; for only through the liberation of Poland can Russians secure national and political freedoms" (31 May 1848) (in Władysław T. Wisłocki, Kongres słowiański w r. 1848 i sprawa polska [Lvov, 1927], p. 49).

70. Lajos Kossuth (1802–1894), lawyer and journalist, championed Magyar opposition to Austrian rule before 1848 and was the key figure in the Hungarian independence movement in 1848–1849. His liberal but intensely nationalistic program denied equal rights with the Magyars to the subject peoples—Croats, Serbs, Romanians, and Slovaks—living in the kingdom of Hungary. After the Hungarian revolution was suppressed by Habsburg and tsarist troops in the summer of 1849, Kossuth escaped and continued to advocate the Magyar cause from exile in England and Italy.

71. Can Bakunin's reconstruction of his message to the Slavs in

Prague be taken at face value? To judge from the protocols, and by his own admission, he took little part in the formal deliberations; but it would have been quite in character for him to expound his views to willing listeners in private, informal gatherings. His strident advocacy of Austria's destruction, however, probably dates from later in 1848, from the period when he wrote the *Appeal to the Slavs;* that is, after Jelačić marched against radical Vienna and Bakunin became convinced that the Habsburg dynasty was succeeding in turning the Slavs into counterrevolutionary cannon fodder.

72. Bakunin's proposal for Slav union ("The Fundamental Principles of the New Slav Policy") first appeared in Polish in the Lvov newspaper *Dziennik Narodowy,* 31 August and 5 September 1848. Czech and German versions were published shortly thereafter. For a translation of Bakunin's French draft, see Lawrence D. Orton, "Bakunin's Plan for Slav Federation, 1848," *Canadian-American Slavic Studies,* VIII (1974), 113–115. Shortly before the congress was disbanded, Bakunin submitted his plan, but the leaders chose not to use it in preparing the official manifestoes. The strongly centralized executive power envisaged by Bakunin was probably intended, as he intimates in the *Confession,* to put an end to the national squabbling among the Slavs.

73. Josip Jelačić (1801–1859), a Croatian nobleman, had been a colonel in the Austrian *Grenzer* (Borderlands) service. Hastily elevated to the rank of general and appointed *ban* (governor) of Croatia by the court and the Croatian diet in March 1848, he led imperial forces against both the Magyars and radical Vienna. European democrats, including Marx and Engels, as well as Bakunin, identified him and the Austrian Slavs as tools of the counterrevolutionary court camarilla.

74. Romanians living in the kingdom of Hungary.

75. The landowners, principally Poles, in the tsarist provinces bordering Galicia displayed great anxiety at the prospect that social unrest might be spreading to their estates. D. G. Bibikov, governor general in Kiev, informed Count Orlov on 27 March (OS) that the Poles "intended to leave their properties during the Easter celebrations and move to the cities." Similarly, M. V. Petrashevskii told a friend in November 1848 that "in the districts bordering Galicia the peasants are in a mood to massacre their landowners." See A. S. Nifontow, *Russland im Jahre 1848* (Berlin, 1953), pp. 158, 195.

76. Because the Dresden jails were overcrowded after the roundup of the May 1849 conspirators, Bakunin was transferred in August to

the Königstein Fortress. The fortress belonged to the ruling Saxon house of Wettin and was located in the picturesque mountain reaches near the Bohemian frontier. In early 1850, after his trial, Bakunin drafted a "Statement of Defense" ("Meine Verteidigung") for the use of his government-appointed attorney, Franz Otto, at the appeal hearing. In this rambling and unfinished document, which Bakunin termed a "political confession," he discoursed at length on the history of Russia since Peter I and on the national question in Austria. The German original is in Václav Čejchan, *Bakunin v Čechách* (Prague, 1928), pp. 101–189; and in Russian translation in Steklov, IV, 31–94.

77. In an angry, chauvinistic, and brilliant poem, "To the Slanderers of Russia," written in 1831 at the time of the Polish uprising, Pushkin reacted to the outcry in Paris concerning aid for the Poles:

> About what are you clamoring, orators of the nations?
> Why with anathema do you threaten Russia?
> What has aroused you? Lithuanian disturbances?
> Stop! This is a quarrel of Slavs among themselves,
>
> . . . . .
>
> Who will prevail in the unequal struggle:
> The haughty Pole or the true Russ?
> Will the Slav streams mingle in the Russian sea?
> Will it dry up? That's the question.

78. Nicholas' note suggests that he took Bakunin's submission at face value. Here, as elsewhere in the *Confession,* Bakunin prefaces with professions of self-abasement and contrition those opinions that were likely to be particularly disagreeable or offensive to the tsar (Nettlau, p. 226).

79. Steklov (IV, 475) maintains that his sentence confirms his supposition that Bakunin had been given a set of specific questions and that these questions were before him as he wrote the *Confession.*

80. The word *khitro,* here translated "cunningly," was used by writers of seventeenth-century Russia in attacking the West. *Khitrost',* "cunning, guile, artfulness" of the West, was contrasted with native Russian *blagochestie,* "piety, faithfulness." Bakunin may be playing, perhaps subconsciously, upon Nicholas' presumed anti-Westernism. For a discussion of *khitrost'* and *blagochestie,* see James H. Billington, *The Icon and the Axe* (New York, 1968), pp. 121–127.

81. This passage on dictatorship is frequently cited by Bakunin's Marxist critics to show that he recognized the need for a centralized revolutionary authority after the victory of the revolution. Victor

Serge, commenting on Bakunin's "prophetic words," wrote: "Lenin himself was unable to explain the Dictatorship of the Proletariat in different words, to contrast it with the democracy of the French and English with greater scorn." Writing in the wake of the October Revolution, Serge maintained that "already in 1848 Bakunin had presaged Bolshevism. This boundless, dictatorial, libertarian power . . . does exist; it is called the Soviet Republic!" (*Forum*, June 1921, p. 377). In reply to Serge, Max Nettlau contended: "The slightest goodwill allows one to see that he [Bakunin] desired, as it were, the technical dictatorship of bootblacking, cleansing soap, and the broom—elementary intellectual, moral, and social hygiene—for a country victimized by colossal negligence" (p. 226). Bakunin's critics on this point are answered at length in Hem Day, "La légende de la dictature chez Bakounine," *La Brochure mensuelle*, nos. 155–156 (November–December 1935), pp. 31–41.

82. These leaders of the French Revolution of 1789 were viewed as demagogues and political opportunists by reactionaries such as Nicholas.

83. Pushkin set out to write a history of the Pugachev Rebellion and was granted access to the secret archives relating to this uprising. He actually started to write his history, of which a few pages have been preserved, but the creative artist in him apparently gained the upper hand (perhaps, like Eugene Onegin, he found no pleasure in "burrowing in the dust of the chronicles of antiquity"), and the result was his masterpiece, *The Captain's Daughter*, from which Bakunin quotes.

84. After the June uprising, Bakunin remained in contact with at least one member of the society, L'udovít Štúr (see n. 96). Another probable member, Josef Václav Frič, leader of the insurgent Prague students, later referred to the society as the "Fraternity of the Slav Future" (*Čech* [Geneva], no. 11 [1861], p. 81).

85. Bakunin alludes here to the change made in the congress agenda midway in the deliberations at the suggestion of Karol Libelt (1807–1875), a Poznań democrat and the chairman of the Polish-Ukrainian section. The new program, which replaced a cumbersome series of discussion questions, called for issuing a manifesto to the European nations, drafting a petition to the emperor containing the demands of the individual Slav nations in the Austrian monarchy, and formulating a plan to further Slav unity. Only the European manifesto was approved by the congress before the sessions were ended by the street fighting that broke out on June 12. The liberal manifesto,

drafted by Palacký, president of the congress, closed prophetically with a summons for a "general European Congress of Nations . . . before the reactionary policy of the individual Courts causes the nations, incited by hatred and malice, mutually to destroy one another." An English translation is in *Slavonic and East European Review*, XXVI, no. 67 (April 1948), 309–313.

86. Military activity in Prague had intensified after 20 May 1848, when General Alfred zu Windischgrätz, a reactionary aristocrat and ardent proponent of Habsburg absolutism, resumed command. Several protest meetings were held, led by the student spokesman J. V. Frič and the radical Czech lawyer Karel Sladkovský. On 12 June a clash between a group of demonstrators and the soldiers in front of the military headquarters led to gunfire (Windischgrätz's wife was mortally wounded) and barricades were thrown up in the narrow streets of the Old Town. The fighting lasted until 17 June, when Windischgrätz dislodged the insurgents by a cannonade from the heights surrounding the city. During the first days of the uprising, Windischgrätz expelled the visiting delegates, thus ending the deliberations of the Slav Congress.

87. Accounts vary concerning Bakunin's activities during the last days of the uprising. He was reported to have been at the insurgents' headquarters in the Clementinum on 15 June in the company of Frič, with whom he was poring over a map of the city (Čejchan, *Bakunin v Čechách*, p. 76 n). J. Šesták reported a conversation between Bakunin and Mayor Vaňka of Prague during the uprising: "Herr Bürgermeister, was ist das für eine Revolution: keine Ordnung, keine Organisation. Jeder macht, was er will!" ("Mr. Mayor, what kind of revolution is this! No order, no organization. Each does as he wishes!") (in Zdeněk V. Tobolka, *Slovanský sjezd v Praze roku 1848* [Prague, 1901], p. 186n). F. Kopp, in *Die Ereignisse der Pfingstwoche des Jahres 1848 und dessen nächster Umgebung* (Prague, 1848), p. 100, wrote of a "general," not Frič, who took command during the bombardment of the insurgents' positions and organized the barricades, impressing everyone with his revolutionary spirit. But Anna Bajerová, who made the most thorough investigation of the uprising, states emphatically that "there cannot be a question of his [Bakunin's] having assumed a measure of command in the Clementinum" (*Svatodušní bouře v Praze r. 1848 ve světle soudního vyšetřování* [Plzen, 1920], pp. 163–164).

88. Indicative of German nationalist (*Grossdeutsch*) opinion toward

the Danubian Slavs was a remark by Ignaz Kuranda in June 1848 in the Leipzig journal *Die Grenzboten:* "Austria had sense and meaning only as a German power; the destiny of Austria was to elevate the primitive Slav peoples [*Naturvölker*] to the level of German civilization, and to offer them as a dowry to Germany." The Germans particularly resented the Czechs' efforts to block elections to the Frankfurt Parliament from Bohemia and Moravia. The German press (including the Viennese) ridiculed the Slav Congress, and initial German press accounts of the June uprising inaccurately characterized the fighting as a national conflict between fanatical ultra-Czechs and Bohemian Germans, and hailed Windischgrätz as the savior of German interests. In a meeting of the Frankfurt Parliament on 20 June, several delegates clamored for the immediate dispatch of Prussian, Saxon, and Bavarian armies (over which the assembly had no authority) to aid their beleaguered German compatriots in Prague and put an end to Slav barbarism. On the hostility of the Frankfurt Parliament toward the Poznanian Poles, see especially Roy Pascal, "The Frankfurt Parliament, 1848, and the *Drang nach Osten*," *Journal of Modern History,* XVIII (1946), 108–122.

89. Immediately upon his arrival in Breslau, Bakunin called on the Democratic Club to issue a pledge of support to the Slav democrats in Prague. Bakunin's proposal precipitated a lengthy and acrimonious debate on the "Slav question" that lasted over several meetings and was finally tabled until it could be ascertained that "the Slavs were in fact democrats." This episode, which made it clear to a disappointed Bakunin that there were no longer European democrats but only German "national" democrats in Breslau, is examined in Pfitzner, "Bakunin und Preussen," pp. 264–269, and in Václav Žáček, *Slovanský sjezd v Praze roku 1848: Sbírka dokumentů* (Prague, 1958), pp. 498–502, where press reports of the club meetings are reproduced.

90. Masaniello was a seventeenth-century Neapolitan revolutionary who became emotionally unbalanced by his successes and was killed by his former supporters.

91. See n. 53. The Russian ambassador at Potsdam, Baron Peter von Meyendorff, in a communication of 15 June 1848 to Prussian Foreign Minister von Arnim, charged that during Bakunin's stay in Breslau in April and May 1848 he became acquainted with the Polish Wychowski brothers. According to Meyendorff, "I am assured that with a sufficiently large sum of money he [Bakunin] would have succeeded in engaging these two individuals to journey under assumed

names to Russia by way of Kraków and Galicia with the aim of making an attempt on the life of the emperor" (Pfitzner, *Bakuninstudien,* p. 58).

92. The accusation, dated Paris, 3 July, by H. Ewerbeck and published in the *Neue Rheinische Zeitung* on 6 July 1848, alleged that George Sand possessed a document that proved Bakunin to be a tsarist agent. Bakunin immediately sent a letter to Sand (apparently not received by her, but published in the Breslau *Allgemeine Oder-Zeitung* on 12 July) demanding that she release the evidence or issue a denial. A second letter from Bakunin reached Sand through Bakunin's friend Reichel. On 20 July Sand replied to both Bakunin and the *Neue Rheinische Zeitung* (printed on 3 August), professing ignorance of the affair, which she called an "infamous and ridiculous calumny." Arnold Ruge, whose *Die Reform* was the principal rival to Marx's newspaper on the German left, in an editorial of 30 July criticized Marx for propagating such an obvious fabrication. Such incidents, it must be said, were not uncommon in the intensely political and not overly scrupulous press of 1848.

93. Drafts of Bakunin's letters of July and August 1848 to *Die Reform, Allgemeine Oder-Zeitung,* and *Neue Rheinische Zeitung* are in Steklov, III, 307–314.

94. Despite financial difficulties and the suspicions and rumors that surrounded him, Bakunin developed close ties with many Silesian and Polish democratic members of the Prussian parliament in Berlin. He shared lodgings with his old friend Hermann Müller-Strübing and resumed his friendship with Arnold Ruge. Ruge had moved *Die Reform* from Breslau to Berlin in August, and he welcomed Bakunin as a collaborator. In September 1848 *Die Reform* was proclaimed the organ of the "Left of the National Assembly."

95. When the republican government closed the National Workshops, barricades sprang up in the poorer sections of Paris. During the June Days the insurgents—the workers and the unemployed, whose social revolution the republican leaders feared—were routed in bloody skirmishes by General Eugène Cavaignac, commander of the Paris National Guard, now swelled by volunteers from the provinces.

96. In a letter of 12 September 1848 from Vienna, Štúr wrote to Bakunin: "Brother, . . . we should be very curious to learn where you are now, why you do not come to us as you promised. We expected you impatiently in Zagreb [where it was hoped that the deliberations of the Slav Congress could be resumed], but when you did not arrive, we thought that something unpleasant had happened to

you. . . . Thank God that is not the case. We . . . are leaving Vienna shortly for the Carpathians on a matter known to you [the planned Slovak rising against the Magyars], and we will await you there as you promised. Come to Slav soil and abandon the German." That Bakunin was less than candid when he dismissed Štúr's letter as "insignificant" is evident in his hastily drafted reply, which was found among his possessions when he was arrested in May 1849: "Brother, what are you doing? You are destroying Slavdom. You have lost your senses; you are sacrificing the great Slav enterprise and acting merely in the interests of the Emperor and the Austrian aristocracy. You believe that diplomacy will save you, but it will destroy you! You have declared war on the revolution; you are serving reaction; you are bringing dishonor on all Slavdom." That Bakunin's dire financial straits may have prevented his journey to Slovakia is implied in his letter of 2 October to an unknown correspondent (in imprecise French): "I have just received a letter from L'udovít Štúr (Slovak); he sends for me and gives me a rendezvous in the Carpathians. I swear to you that I would very much like to go there, not only in order to understand better the very tangled Slav question; besides, I am convinced that I will be able to contribute to giving him a more rational and more liberal direction; these gentlemen have confidence in me. In Prague we agreed on all the main points; it would be my duty to go there, and although I am here I cannot find a free moment because my friends from Russia, instead of money, up to now send me only promises and kind words" (Polonskii, *Materialy*, I, 28; Steklov, III, 320, 323–324, 516–517; Čejchan, *Bakunin v Čechách*, pp. 33–35, 78n).

97. Bakunin's second expulsion from Berlin was remarkably similar to his ordeal in April. On 21 September he was interrogated by Chief of Police Bardeleben (Minutoli was by then a special Prussian envoy to England), who ordered his immediate departure. The Berlin authorities, who had tolerated Bakunin's presence throughout the summer, were goaded into this action by the mounting insistence of the tsarist goverment, culminating in a report by von Rochow, the Prussian ambassador in St. Petersburg, who urged Bakunin's expulsion "under any sort of pretext" in order to preserve amicable diplomatic relations. Arriving in Breslau on 23 September, Bakunin was arrested, despite his attempt at disguise, and was expelled on 6 October, with the threat of being handed over to the Russians if he failed to leave Prussian territory. He then went to Dresden, but the Saxon officials, equally unwilling to antagonize Russia, expelled him, on the pretext of a tsarist request for his extradition in 1844. Finally, on 11 October,

Bakunin found a haven in Köthen. His harassment by the Prussian and Saxon authorities drew loud protests from the democratic German press (e.g., Ruge's *Reform*, the Breslau *Allgemeine Oder-Zeitung*, the *Dresdner Zeitung*, and even Marx's *Neue Rheinische Zeitung*), but to no avail, for the conservative elements were regaining the upper hand. See Pfitzner, *Bakuninstudien*, especially chap. 6, "Bakunins Ausweisung aus Preussen und Sachsen."

98. The Duchy of Anhalt (approximately 100,000 inhabitants at mid-century) was divided until 1863 into the politically autonomous city-states of Anhalt-Bernburg and Anhalt-Köthen. As Bakunin states, the constitutionally liberal enclave of Köthen became a haven for democratic refugees as the tide of reaction mounted in neighboring Prussia and Saxony in the latter half of 1848.

99. In August, soon after the court left Innsbruck for Vienna, war erupted in Hungary between the imperial forces, supported by the Austro-Slavs, and the Magyar separatists. When Jelačić advanced his Croatian troops against Budapest in September, German nationalist and radical opinion in Vienna sided with the Magyars. Popular wrath focused on the minister of war, Count Latour, who had been supplying arms and money to the Croatians. On 6 October, ostensibly to halt reinforcements for Jelačić, a mob stormed the war ministry and hanged Latour. The next day the court again fled, this time to the provincial Moravian town of Olomouc. Jelačić, now placed under Windischgrätz's command, interrupted his march on Budapest to subdue Vienna. The inner city was captured on 31 October, martial law was proclaimed, and the insurgent leaders were executed.

100. The suggestion that Bakunin appeal to the Slavs came in a letter of 19 October (that is, while Jelačić was besieging radical Vienna, to the delight of the Czech moderates) from his radical Berlin acquaintance Hermann Müller-Strübing: "How terribly your friends the Czechs are behaving! Fulminate against this you must! A Slav must speak out for democracy and must thoroughly brand these perfidious paladins of nationality with their mendacious royalism. . . . You have to break openly with them. Make an appeal to the democrats among the Slavs" (*Pfitzner, Bakuninstudien*, p. 92). Here was an irresistible challenge: to redirect the Danubian Slavs, whom Bakunin, since the days of the Slav Congress, had viewed paternally as delightful but misguided children. To shield Ernst Keil, his publisher and the owner of the Slav bookstore in Leipzig, the frontispiece of the brochure stated: "*Appeal to the Slavs by a Russian Patriot*, Mikhail Bakunin, Member of the Slav Congress in Prague. Published by the

Author in Köthen." The thirty-five-page German version, prepared by Müller-Strübing from Bakunin's French draft, appeared in December 1848. It is reprinted in Bakunin, "Zwei Schriften aus der 40er Jahren des XIX. Jahrhunderts," *Internationale Bibliothek für Philosophie,* II, no. 11/12 (Prague, 1936), 23–43. A Russian version is in Steklov, III, 345–366; brief excerpts in English are in *Bakunin on Anarchy,* ed. Sam Dolgoff (New York, 1972), pp. 63–68.

101. Frederick William IV summarily adjourned the Prussian parliament on 9 November and ordered it to the provincial town of Brandenburg. Soon after, this body was dissolved and a new constitution was proclaimed. Of the two radical Germans that Bakunin mentions, only the Cologne democrat Karl d'Ester (1811–1859) was actually a member of the Prussian parliament. Contrary to what Bakunin says, he had made the acquaintance of d'Ester (who belonged to Marx's circle of communists) in 1845 in Brussels. After the triumph of the counterrevolution in 1849, d'Ester emigrated to Switzerland. Karl Hexamer, who was active in radical journalistic enterprises in 1848–1849, later emigrated to America.

102. Aroused from inactivity and despondency by the challenge of writing the *Appeal to the Slavs,* and increasingly restless in the provincial confines of Köthen, Bakunin journeyed to Leipzig on 30 December 1848. A further reason for his journey was to arrange with Keil for a Polish translation of the *Appeal.* Suspicious of the Saxon authorities, Bakunin did not register with the police in Leipzig, as was required, and he changed his lodgings frequently.

103. Bakunin had met Gustav Straka in Prague in June 1848. In Leipzig he lodged briefly with the brothers, who became his principal source of information on developments in Bohemia and his go-between with the Czech radicals. The Straka brothers were later indicted and sentenced (Adolf *in absentia*) for their part in the May 1849 conspiracy in Prague. Gustav's testimony figures prominently at Bakunin's trial in Austria in 1851. See Polonskii, *Materialy,* I, 75–78.

104. Karel Sabina (1811–1877) founded and edited several radical Czech newspapers in 1848–1849. He was arrested in conjunction with the May 1849 conspiracy in Bohemia and interned in Austrian jails until 1857. In later years, a destitute Sabina actually became an informer for the Austrian police.

The *Appeal* was published in Czech in its entirety—not just "an excerpt," as Bakunin states—in *Noviny Lípy Slovanské* (News of the Slav Linden), nos. 1–4 (2–5 January 1849). Although Sabina had deleted from the Czech version a defamatory characterization of Emperor Ferdinand as a "pitiful, imbecile creature who is pushed hither and yon by females and courtiers," suppression of the *Appeal* was justified according to the temporary Austrian press code of 1848. But the censors were adjusting to new procedures and therefore failed to act before the last installment appeared on 5 January. Sabina was saved by the statement of dissociation appended to this final installment. The publication in Prague of Bakunin's call for the destruction of Austria understandably created a stir; the *Prager Zeitung* exploited the incident to indict the entire Czech national movement (not just Sabina and the radicals), which it held accountable for Bakunin's opinions, since he had proudly identified himself as a member of the Czech-sponsored Slav Congress on the title page of his brochure. Put on the defensive, the leading Czech spokesmen, František Palacký and Karel Havlíček, hastily dissociated themselves from Bakunin's views. The press polemic that Sabina's action had launched led to a sharper distinction between the Czech radicals and liberals (perhaps this was Sabina's intention in publishing the *Appeal*), and was a foretaste of the government's abandonment of the Czech moderates who had supported the floundering monarchy during 1848, much as Bakunin had predicted. On the *Appeal*'s impact in Bohemia, see Josef Kočí, "Česká politika a Bakuninův 'Hlas k Slovanům,' " *Slovanské historické studie*, X (1974), 113–140.

105. Emanuel Arnold (1801–1869), Czech littérateur and an active participant in the Czech revolution, in November 1848 founded *Občanské Noviny* (Citizens' News), whose message was directed primarily to the peasantry. Arnold also was arrested after the May 1849 conspiracy and imprisoned until 1857.

106. Founded in Prague on 30 April 1848 and soon spreading throughout the Austro-Slav lands, Slovanská Lípa (Slav Linden Society) fostered national and political consciousness among the Slavs. The society's program, issued on 24 May, emphasized the defense of newly won constitutional liberties and the securing of national equality in education and government, and pledged itself to promote commerce and industry in predominantly Slav regions of the monarchy. It launched a newspaper of the same name on 2 October; on 2 January 1849, when the paper became a daily, the name was changed to *Noviny Lípy Slovanské*. Originally headed by moderate Austro-Slavs (Šafařík was its first president), the society was increasingly dominated by Czech radicals by the second half of 1848. In December the society held a widely publicized congress of its affiliates in Prague, to the an-

noyance of the Austrian authorities; but by spring 1849 the society had become a casualty of the victorious counterrevolution. Professor Stanley Pech, in *The Czech Revolution of 1848* (Chapel Hill, N.C., 1969), lauded the society as "the first political organization of the Czechs—and the finest political-institutional product of the revolutionary era" (p. 345).

107. Either Bakunin's memory lapsed or he deliberately sought to conceal from Nicholas his earlier acquaintance with Sabina, whom he first met at the Slav Congress. (In his Saxon prison deposition he admitted that he had made Sabina's acquaintance in Prague, but "only in passing.") Before Bakunin left Köthen for Leipzig, however, he had expressly directed that a copy of the *Appeal* be sent to Sabina. See Steklov, IV, 496.

108. In the years before 1848 Prague had become a center of the Slav revival. Slav scholars chose Prague as a place to study, conduct research, and publish their work. Despite the city's outward German appearance and character, a mythology about the city as a citadel of Slav history and culture had grown up among Slav enthusiasts. The Slovene Stanko Vraz, writing in 1844 to a Czech acquaintance, K. J. Erben, extolled this city "where, from each street, each palace and home, yes, each stone, Slav history speaks forth in golden tongues, and in which . . . Slav reciprocity, accompanied by a genial erudition, ascends to its golden throne" (Tobolka, *Slovanský sjezd,* pp. 50–51).

109. Nettlau (pp. 229–230) points to "an astonishing continuity of ideas and even of expressions" running through Bakunin's writings. This passage on directing the revolution against things rather than individuals reappears in remarkably similar phrasing in 1869 in Bakunin's "Program of the International Brotherhood (Secret Alliance)": "Therefore, to make a successful revolution, it is necessary to attack conditions and material goods; to destroy property and the State. It will then become unnecessary to destroy men and be condemned to suffer the sure and inevitable reaction which no massacre has ever failed and ever will fail to produce in every society" (Dolgoff, *Bakunin on Anarchy,* p. 151).

110. Count László Teleki (1811–1861) and Lajos Batthyány led the liberal Magyar magnates who before 1848 supported Kossuth's opposition to centrist rule from Vienna. Teleki's mission for Kossuth in Paris was to gain formal French recognition of the Hungarian revolutionary government. The Austrian ambassador in Paris threatened that Austria would view recognition and the sending of a French

envoy to Pest as a *casus belli*. After the Magyar defeat at Világos in August 1849, Teleki joined Kossuth in exile. In May 1861 he committed suicide.

111. The *Appeal* was serialized (but not completed) in Flocon's *La Reforme*, nos. 1, 3, 6, 13 (1, 4, 7, 14 January 1849). The introduction (by Flocon?) to the first installment praised it as "a work of courage and energy," and added that "we admire Bakunin even if we deem his policy a dream." The *Appeal* was also discussed in Proudhon's Paris daily, *Le Peuple*, no. 50 (7 January 1849), in a lead article, "Le Panslavisme." Excerpts and favorable commentary were published in Paris in the Polish émigré journal *Demokrata Polski* (17 February 1849).

112. Again Bakunin is less than candid. "We know that in Leipzig, Berlin, Breslau, and Dresden he attended German meetings, met with German political figures, and even gathered several of them around him"; but it is true that the Germans and their plans interested Bakunin only in conjunction with his Slav plans (Steklov, IV, 500–501).

113. There is little evidence of any significant change in German public opinion toward the Slavs in early 1849. An indication of Bakunin's delusion that German Slav-baiting was lessening can be found in Marx's *Neue Rheinische Zeitung*. In a critique of the *Appeal*, Friedrich Engels ridiculed the pretensions to nationhood of the "unhistorical" Danubian Slavs (Czechs, Slovaks, Croats, Slovenes), who were "necessarily counterrevolutionary" and whose national demise was inevitable. Such words were hardly indicative of a rapprochement between the Slav and German democrats. See "Der demokratische Panslavismus," *Neue Rheinische Zeitung*, nos. 222–223 (15–16 February 1849); English translation in Karl Marx, *Political Writings*, I: *The Revolutions of 1848*, ed. David Fernbach (Middlesex, England, 1973), 226–245. Cf. Roman Rosdolsky, "Friedrich Engels und das Problem der 'Geschichtslosen Völker': Die Nationalitätenfrage in der Revolution 1848–49 im Lichte der 'Neuen Rheinischen Zeitung,' " *Archiv für Sozialgeschichte*, IV (1964), especially 215–239.

114. Bakunin grossly overestimates the ability of d'Ester and Hexamer, not to mention his own, to dampen the rising national passions that were spreading throughout Central Europe in 1848–1849. Their efforts were inconsequential when measured against developments in Hungary (where Croats, Serbs, Slovaks, and even Romanians fought pitched battles with the Magyars), no less than against the sentiments expressed in the Frankfurt Parliament and the German press denouncing the Slavs as tools of the counterrevolution (Nettlau, p. 230).

115. At the time that he was interrogated in Austria, Arnold main-

tained that his conversation with Bakunin was mainly about socialism, and that Bakunin tried to persuade him to agitate for the cause
of socialism in Bohemia. Bakunin denied the charge, claiming that
Arnold had distorted and misunderstood their exchange, and that the
essential points he had raised with Arnold were the need to win the
support of the Slav Linden Society and to synchronize the timing of
the Slav revolution with the outbreak in Germany (Čejchan, *Bakunin
v Čechách*, pp. 41–42).

116. Charles-Alain-Gabriel de Rohan, Prince of Guémenée and
Duke of Montbazon (1764–1836), scion of an ancient Breton noble
family, emigrated during the Revolution of 1789 and entered the Austrian military service, rising to the rank of field marshal. Even after
the Restoration he rarely visited France, preferring to live on his Bohemian estate at Sichrow, where Arnold had been in his service.

117. Oswald Ottendorfer (1825–?), a Viennese student from Zwit-
tau (Svitavy) in Moravia, participated in the March 1848 revolution in
Vienna and fought the Danes in Schleswig-Holstein. Bakunin first
met him in Breslau in May 1848. Ottendorfer joined the October insurrection in Vienna and escaped to Germany when Jelačić stormed
the capital. After the May 1849 conspiracy in Bohemia failed, he took
part in the South German "Second Revolution" and then emigrated to
America.

118. This passage prompted Steklov (IV, 504) to remark: "Here Bakunin openly admits that he has earmarked for himself the role of
dictator in the event of a radical revolution—and correctly so, since
there was no one else in his circle capable of it." Cf. n. 81 In a less
flattering assessment, Carr quotes this passage as evidence of the
"first of that strange series of half-real, half-imaginary secret societies
of which Bakunin's brain became, in his later years, so prolific. . . .
It is a characteristic blend of megalomania, vanity, and naïve dis-
ingenuousness. . . . In theory a protagonist of absolute liberty, and
ready both now and later to denounce in the bitterest terms the rigid
discipline of communism, Bakunin resorted, in the organization of
his revolutionary activities, to methods which were not only the pre-
cise contradiction of his own principles, but went far beyond the
most extreme ambitions of the dogmatic and dictatorial Marx. It was
an inconsistency which never seems for a moment to have troubled
Bakunin's mind. He could preach unrestrained liberty as a social and
political principle, while demanding from his disciples 'unconditional obedience' to his own will" (*Michael Bakunin* [New York, 1961],
pp. 192–193).

119. Bakunin is mistaken. A Polish branch of the Slovanská Lípa (Związek Filialny Pragskiej Lipy Słowiańskiej) was founded in Lvov in August 1848 by the pro-Slav lawyer Karol Malisz. The Galician affiliate exchanged greetings and letters with the parent society in Prague. The correspondence was published in *Lípa Slovanská*, nos. 1 and 2 (2 and 5 October 1848), pp. 3 and 6–7.

120. Bakunin accurately describes the purpose and tenor of Jelačić's letter, but fails to mention that the Prague Slovanská Lípa replied publicly to the Croatian *ban* expressing their appreciation of his defense of Slav interests and pledging to support him. In October the Czech radicals still held a minority position in the Slovanská Lípa. Both letters were printed in *Lípa Slovanská*, no. 8 (26 October 1848), pp. 29–30.

121. Kossuth and the Magyars received popular support in Bohemia and Moravia in the spring of 1849, but not because of any change in German press opinion, as Bakunin maintained on p. 116, or as a result of his two *Appeals;* Czech support of Kossuth came primarily because of reports of Russian intervention in Hungary and after the dissolution of the Austrian parliament in Kroměříž on 6 March. See Pech, *Czech Revolution of 1848*, pp. 251–252.

122. Heimberger was a violin student at the Leipzig Conservatory. Bakunin met him at one of the many student gatherings. A self-styled Polish patriot, Heimberger changed his name to Lassogórski. Richard Wagner recalls encountering Bakunin and the zealous but frightened Heimberger at the peak of the Dresden uprising: "Now that Haimberger [sic] had shouldered a gun, and presented himself for service at the barricades, . . . Bakunin had greeted him none the less joyfully. He had drawn him down to sit by his side on the couch, and every time the youth shuddered with fear at the violent sound of the cannon-shot, he slapped him vigorously on the back and cried out: 'You are not in the company of your fiddle here, my friend. What a pity you didn't stay where you were!'" (*My Life* [London, 1911], p. 491).

123. The press reports in February and March 1849 that Russian forces had crossed onto Austrian soil to join the fighting against the Magyars were exaggerated; in fact, only one small detachment had entered Transylvania at that time. The *Second Appeal to the Slavs* was also directed at the Czechs, and this time Bakunin urged the Slavs to rid themselves of their treacherous leaders—Jelačić, Rajačić (the Serbian primate), and Palacký—who have "sold you out to the Austrian dynasty and Nicholas." A few copies that crossed the border

prompted the Austrian authorities to add a new set of charges against
Bakunin. The German text is in Čejchan, *Bakunin v Čechách*, pp.
193–200; a Russian version is in Steklov, III, 372–379.

124. Ludwig Wittig (1815–?), Saxon journalist and political radical,
first met Bakunin in 1842. In April 1849, as editor of the democratic
Dresdner Zeitung, Wittig gave space to Bakunin for a series of articles
entitled "Russische Zustände" (Russian Conditions). When Bakunin
speaks of the German press adopting a more sympathetic attitude
toward the Slav democrats, he undoubtedly has in mind the *Dresdner
Zeitung*. See B. Nikolajewsky, "M. A. Bakunin in der 'Dresdner
Zeitung,' " *International Review for Social History*, I (1936), 121–216;
and Pfitzner, *Bakuninstudien*, chap. 9: "Bakunin und die *Dresdner
Zeitung*." After the Dresden revolt was suppressed in May 1849, Wittig fought in the Baden insurrection, then emigrated from Germany.

125. August Röckel (1814–1876), music director at the Saxon court,
supported the republican cause in 1848 in political pamphlets and in
the radical weekly *Volksblätter*, which he edited. It was Röckel that introduced Bakunin to Richard Wagner. Röckel was arrested and tried
with Bakunin for their part in the May 1849 Dresden uprising. He
was not freed until 1862.

126. Aleksander Krzyżanowski (1819–?) emigrated to France from
Galicia in 1842. In 1848 the émigré Polish Democratic Society sent
him back to Austrian Poland to assist Wiktor Heltman (see n. 127).
After the Baden insurrection collapsed in the summer of 1849, Krzyżanowski escaped to Switzerland.

127. Wiktor Heltman (1796–1874) was arrested in the 1820s for his
outspoken Polish patriotism and was impressed into the Russian military service. He deserted in 1831 and fought briefly in the Polish insurrection before emigrating to France. A prolific publicist for the
Polish cause, he was a member of the executive Centralizacja (see n.
37) of the Polish Democratic Society. In the 1840s he organized Polish
conspiracies in the Duchy of Poznań and Galicia. After the March
1848 revolution he returned to Kraków and Galicia, where he was active in the revolutionary movement until he was forced to flee from
the Austrian authorities after the abortive Lvov uprising in November. After a brief stay in Paris he returned to Central Europe with
Krzyżanowski to coordinate the Polish and German revolutionary
activities. Following the setbacks of 1849 he withdrew from
revolutionary activity and settled in Brussels, where he devoted himself to literary and historical study.

128. Informing only Arnold and Heimberger of his intentions, Ba-

kunin traveled secretly to Prague at the end of March, using a British passport issued in the name of Andersson that Krzyżanowski had supplied.

129. The meeting with the Czechs was held at the home of the Prague lawyer Karel Preiss, with whom Bakunin was staying. Bakunin's advice to the Czech radicals echoed the arguments in the *Appeal:* The Czechs must join the German and Magyar democrats; they must cease theorizing and lay concrete plans for insurrection; and their goal must be the destruction of the Austrian state (Čejchan, *Bakunin v Čechách,* pp. 46–48).

130. During his four days in Prague, Bakunin changed his lodgings frequently to avoid detection, and he was annoyed to learn that his presence had become common knowledge among the Czech politicians. After the publication of the first *Appeal to the Slavs* in Sabina's newspaper, the state prosecutor had ordered the confiscation of all copies of the brochure in Prague bookshops—twenty-three were taken—and directed that Bakunin be arrested if he crossed into Austrian territory. No basis for legal action against Sabina or the *Noviny Lípy Slovanské* was found. See Václav Čejchan, "Bakuninova 'Provolání k Slovanům' před tiskovým soudem pražským r. 1849," *Slovanský přehled,* XXIII (1931), 664–684.

131. Friedrich Baier (1810–1850) was introduced to Bakunin by Wittig on the eve of the Dresden uprising. Baier had commanded the Leopoldstadt (Lipótvár, Leopoldov) Fortress in present-day Slovakia.

132. Their correspondence was addressed in care of a third party and was written partially in cipher. Frič, for example, was "C. Z."

133. Bakunin, perhaps purposely, neglects to mention Józef Akkort, a Kraków Pole, who was his emissary in Prague. During his Saxon and Austrian interrogations, Bakunin minimized Akkort's role, implying that Akkort went to Prague unwillingly. Bakunin also fails to mention that Akkort brought the Czech student leader J. V. Frič to Dresden to confer on plans for an insurrection in Prague. On Röckel's mission to Prague, see n. 144.

134. Eduard von Reichenbach (1812–1869), a descendant of the Silesian landed nobility, embraced radical republicanism. He was elected to the Prussian Assembly in 1848.

135. Prosper-Léon Duvergier de Hauranne (1798–1881), French littérateur, journalist, and politician, supported Thiers' opposition to Guizot's rule in the 1840s. Active in the banquet campaigns of 1847–1848, he nevertheless turned against the Second Republic. Du-

vergier was known as a clever politician and a brilliant debater in the assembly, but he was also considered a political chameleon.

136. The last gasp of the German revolution occurred in the traditional southwestern center of German radicalism, the Bavarian Palatinate and the Duchy of Baden. Radicals from Central Europe, particularly Poles and Magyars, flocked to Baden in May and June 1849 to support the local insurgents. As was the case in Dresden, the revolts in the Palatinate and Baden were eventually suppressed by Prussian troops.

137. Eduard Theodor Jäkel (or Jaeckel) (1817–1874) was a radical Saxon journalist, a republican, and a principal organizer of the Vaterlandsvereine (Patriotic Associations), which were a major voice of the political left. In April 1849 the general assembly of the Vaterlandsvereine met in Dresden. Delegates from 218 associations representing 75,000 members participated. Jäkel, Tzschirner (see n. 138), and the Chemnitz republican Carl Böttcher were elected to the new three-man Central Committee.

Polonskii is mistaken in saying that Bakunin refers to Röckel here. (His error is repeated in the French, German, and Czech translations.) Perhaps the cause of the confusion is Bakunin's ambiguity in failing to make a clear distinction between the two separate central committees of German democrats. The first, consisting of d'Ester, Hexamer, and Reichenbach, was the former Berlin Central Committee of the All-German Democracy, which had moved to Leipzig after the victory of the counterrevolution in Prussia at the end of 1848. The second was the Central Committee of the Vaterlandsvereine, elected in April 1849. See Rolf Weber, *Die Revolution in Sachsen 1848/49* (Berlin, 1970), pp. 276–277.

138. Samuel Erdmann Tzschirner (1812–1870), a lawyer from Bautzen, was a member of the popularly elected (December 1848) Second Chamber of the Saxon Landtag. A spokesman for the extreme left, Tzschirner was appointed to the revolutionary Saxon Provisional Government on 5 May 1849. After the Dresden insurrection failed, he fought in Baden and later escaped abroad.

139. Bakunin was closely acquainted with several other Germans in Dresden whom he did not mention in the *Confession*, most notably Richard Wagner, who recorded his first encounter with Bakunin in *My Life:* "I was immediately struck by his singular and altogether imposing personality. He was in the full bloom of manhood, anywhere between thirty and forty years of age. Everything about him was

colossal, and he was full of a primitive exuberance and strength. . . . His general mode of discussion was the Socratic method, and he seemed quite at his ease when, stretched on his host's [Röckel's] hard sofa, he could argue discursively with a crowd of all sorts of men on the problems of revolution. . . . It was impossible to triumph against his opinions, stated as they were with the utmost conviction, and overstepping in every direction even the extremest bounds of radicalism [p. 467]. . . . in this remarkable man the purest impulses of an ideal humanity conflicted strangely with a savagery entirely inimical to all civilisation, so that my feelings during my intercourse with him fluctuated between involuntary horror and irresistible attraction [p. 470]."

140. Dr. Erbe was a lawyer from Altenburg in Saxony.

141. Franciszek Sznajde (1790–1850), a cavalry commander during the 1830 Polish insurrection, emigrated to France, where he was appointed to the executive Centralizacja of the Polish Democratic Society. He and his fellow Pole Ludwik Mierosławski played important roles in the May 1849 Baden uprising.

142. The Frankfurt constitution for a united Germany, which called for a constitutional monarchy excluding the Habsburg lands, was passed on 27 March with the combined support of the *kleindeutsch* liberals and the radicals. It stipulated a single legislative chamber elected by universal direct suffrage. The next day the parliament voted to offer the crown to the king of Prussia. He refused it, stating that he would accept the crown only if it were offered by the princes. Privately the Hohenzollern ruler expressed his disgust for a "crown offered him by bakers and butchers, and reeking with the stench of the revolution."

143. The Saxon government split over the Frankfurt constitution, and the king rejected it after receiving assurances of military support from Prussia. On 28 April the Saxon ruler dissolved the Landtag, where there was strong pro-Frankfurt sentiment.

144. Apparently disdaining the role of go-between and messenger, Röckel took to Prague neither the letters of introduction nor the messages given him by Bakunin. (They were found when Röckel was arrested after returning to Dresden, and were used as evidence at Bakunin's trial in Austria.) One of Bakunin's aims in sending Röckel to Prague was to demonstrate to the Czechs that not all Germans were rabid anti-Slavs. Röckel's visit was cut short when he learned on 5 May of the outbreak of the Dresden revolution and hurried home. The insurrection in Prague, however, never came to pass; during the

night of 9–10 May, the very time of Bakunin's arrest in Chemnitz, the Prague authorities struck against the leaders of the Bohemian "conspiracy" before they could launch their plan.

145. Karl Zimmer, Sudeten German democrat and a physician by profession, played an active part in all phases of the 1848–1849 revolution in the Austrian lands. Implicated in the abortive May 1849 conspiracy in Prague, he was arrested in March 1850 by the Prussian authorities in Berlin and extradited to Austria, where he was tried with Bakunin and sentenced to fifteen years' imprisonment.

146. On 30 April, two days after dissolving the Landtag, Friedrich August II of Saxony dismissed three ministers who had favored the Frankfurt constitution, thereby precipitating a political crisis. Mass meetings and demonstrations turned into outright insurrection on 3 May when it was learned that Count Friedrich von Beust, the Saxon foreign minister, had requested Prussian military aid to restore order. Barricades were erected and the arsenal was attacked. A revolutionary committee of public safety (*Sicherheitsausschuss*) was formed to plan resistance to the foreign troops. The next morning the king fled to the Königstein Fortress (where Bakunin would later be interned).

147. Bakunin's claim that he took no part in the first days of the Dresden uprising and was contemptuous of its organization is supported by Wagner, who recalled that, as he was making his way to the town hall on the morning of 4 May, his "attention was suddenly distracted by my seeing Bakunin emerge from his hiding-place, and wander among the barricades in a black frockcoat. But I was very much mistaken in thinking he would be pleased with what he saw; he recognised the childish inefficiency of all the measures that had been taken for defence, and declared that the only satisfaction he could feel in the state of affairs was that he need not trouble about the police, but could calmly consider the question of going elsewhere, as he found no inducement to take part in an insurrection conducted in such a slovenly fashion. . . . he walked about smoking his cigar, and making fun of the *naïveté* of the Dresden revolution" (*My Life*, p. 478).

148. Otto Leonhard Heubner (1812–1893), a lawyer and writer with moderate leftist political views, introduced the *Turnen* (gymnastics) movement of Friedrich Ludwig (Father) Jahn into Saxony in 1833. In 1848–1849 Heubner was a member of both the Saxon Landtag and the Frankfurt Parliament. Arrested with Bakunin in Chemnitz in May 1849, he was tried and sentenced to death. The sentence was later

commuted to life imprisonment and in 1859 he was granted amnesty. He later re-entered politics in Saxony.

Carl Gotthelf Todt (1803–1852), a moderate liberal who led the pre-March opposition in the Saxon Landtag, was introduced to Bakunin in 1841 by Arnold Ruge. After the suppression of the Dresden uprising he fled to Switzerland.

149. The extent of Bakunin's leadership of the Dresden uprising, like that of his involvement with the Prague uprising, was disputed by his contemporaries. Count von Waldersee, commander of the Prussian forces besieging Dresden, and, later, the Saxon investigative authorities maintained that Bakunin established complete control over the provisional government and was in effect the dictator of the revolution. The writer Stephan Born, who commanded the barricades during the last days of the fighting, described Bakunin's role as minimal and ineffectual. Wagner wrote that Bakunin maintained a "wonderful sangfroid" throughout the hostilities, calmly giving advice and issuing instructions along with the Polish officers he had assembled. On the conflicting opinions regarding Bakunin's role in the fighting, see especially Steklov, IV, 536–546.

150. Alexander Clarus Heinze had earlier served in the Greek army. He was taken prisoner by the Prussians on 7 May, at the height of the fighting. Bakunin's bitter denunciation of Heinze and his failure even to mention Heinze's successor, Stephan Born, may be partly due to the jealousies and differences among the revolutionary leaders, especially as the situation deteriorated.

151. Nettlau reports (pp. 231–232) on a letter he received in 1894 from a Dr. Enno Sander, who wrote from St. Louis, Missouri, that as a young soldier he had guided Tzschirner and the Poles Heltman and Krzyżanowski to a remote rail station, whence he and the Poles (Tzschirner apparently having decided to return to Dresden) reached safety in Anhalt-Köthen. All three later fought in Baden, and Sander subsequently emigrated to the United States.

152. Wagner confirms that Heubner's courage played a key role in Bakunin's decision to remain in Dresden despite the dim chances of success: "Heubner . . . , without a weapon to defend himself, and with bared head, jumped immediately on to the top of the barricade, which had just been abandoned by all its defenders. He was the sole member of the provisional government to remain on the spot. . . . Heubner turned round to exhort the volunteers to advance, addressing them in stirring words. His success was complete, the barricade

was taken again, . . . the troops . . . were forced to retire. Bakunin had been in close touch with this action, . . . and he now explained to me that however narrow might be the political views of Heubner . . . , he was a man of noble character, at whose service he had immediately placed his own life. Bakunin had only needed this example to determine his own line of conduct; he had decided to risk his neck in the attempt and to ask no further questions" (*My Life*, p. 482). Bakunin's defense of Heubner in the *Confession* may also have been calculated to ease Heubner's punishment. Whereas Todt and Tzschirner had escaped to Switzerland, Heubner still languished in a Saxon prison.

153. The principal buildings destroyed by fire were the old opera house (according to Wagner a firetrap and an eyesore) and a small portion of the Zwinger. Wagner also confirms Bakunin's wish to blow up the town hall, which undoubtedly contributed to the widely held view of Bakunin as the fanatical dictator determined to raze Dresden. "Bakunin had now proposed that all the powder stores should be brought together in the lower rooms of the Town Hall, and that on the approach of the enemy it should be blown up. The town council . . . had remonstrated with the greatest vehemence. Bakunin, however, had insisted . . . on the execution of the measure, but in the end had been completely outwitted by the removal of all the powder stores. Moreover, Heubner, to whom Bakunin could refuse nothing, had been won over to the other side" (*My Life*, p. 492).

154. Again it is Wagner who, having arrived in Chemnitz just after Bakunin and the provisional government, provides details of their betrayal and arrest: "Heubner, Bakunin, and the man called Martin . . . had, it seemed, arrived before me in a hackney-coach at the gates of Chemnitz. On being asked for their names Heubner had announced himself in a tone of authority, and had bidden the town councillors come to him at a certain hotel. They had no sooner reached the hotel than they all three collapsed from excessive fatigue. Suddenly the police broke into the room and arrested them in the name of the local government, upon which they only begged to have a few hours' quiet sleep, pointing out that flight was out of the question in their present condition. I heard further that they had been removed to Altenburg under a strong military escort. . . . the Chemnitz municipal guard, which had been forced to start for Dresden much against its will, and had resolved at the very outset to place itself at the disposal of the royal forces on arriving there, had deceived

Heubner by inviting him to Chemnitz, and had lured him into the trap" (*My Life*, p. 499).

155. Robert Blum (1807–1848), a gifted orator and leader of the Saxon liberals before 1848, was elected to the Frankfurt Parliament, where he was a spokesman of the democratic left. Blum went to Vienna with Julius Fröbel (see n. 9) in October 1848, bearing an address of support from Frankfurt to the Viennese insurgents. Embroiled in the fighting there, he was captured and executed by the victorious counterrevolutionary forces. His execution signaled the final breach between Frankfurt and the Austrian court, and the indignation and sorrow expressed in the democratic press made Blum into a martyr.

INDEX

The *Confession* of
Mikhail Bakunin

Designed by R. E. Rosenbaum.
Composed by Vail-Ballou Press, Inc ,
in 10 point VIP Palatino, 2 points leaded,
with display lines in Palatino.
Printed offset by Vail-Ballou Press
Warren's No. 66 text, 50 pound basis.
Bound by Vail-Ballou Press
in Joanna book cloth
and stamped in All Purpose foil.

Library of Congress Cataloging in Publication Data
(For library cataloging purposes only)

Bakunin, Mikhail Aleksandrovich, 1814–1876.
  The confession of Mikhail Bakunin.

  Translation of Ispoved'.
  Includes bibliographical references and index.
  1. Bakunin, Mikhail Aleksandrovich, 1814–1876. 2. Anarchism and
anarchists—Biography. I. Orton, Lawrence D. II. Title.
HX915.B22313   335'.83'0924 [B]   76 25646
ISBN 0-8014-1073-8

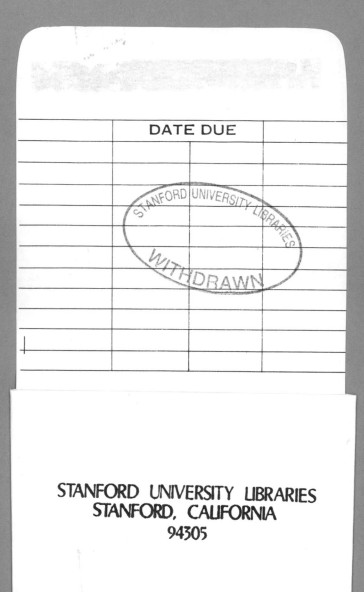